A JUST AND HOLY CAUSE?

MERCER UNIVERSITY

MERCER UNIVERSITY PRESS

Endowed by

TOM WATSON BROWN
and
THE WATSON-BROWN FOUNDATION, INC.

A JUST AND HOLY CAUSE?

The Civil War Letters of
Marcus Bethune and Martha Frances Ely
1862–1865

Edited by Linda S. McCardle

Mercer University Press | MACON, GEORGIA
2016

MUP/ H915

Published by Mercer University Press
1501 Mercer University Drive
Macon, Georgia 31207

9 8 7 6 5 4 3 2 1

Books published by Mercer University Press are printed on acid-free paper that meets the requirements of the American National Standard for Information Sciences—Permanence of Paper for Printed Library Materials.

The images belong to family of the editor.
The bible and letters are the personal property of the editor.

Library of Congress Cataloging-in-Publication Data

Names: Ely, Marcus Bethune, 1831-1880. | Ely, Martha Frances, 1834-1924, author. | McCardle, Linda S., 1953- editor.
Title: A just and holy cause? : the Civil War letters of Marcus Bethune and Martha Frances Ely, 1862-1865 / edited by Linda S. McCardle.
Description: Macon, Georgia : Mercer University Press, 2016. | Includes bibliographical references and index.
Identifiers: LCCN 2016009372 | ISBN 9780881465693 (hardback : alk. paper)
Subjects: LCSH: Ely, Marcus Bethune, 1831-1880--Correspondence. | Confederate States of America. Army. Georgia Infantry Regiment, 54th. | United States--History--Civil War, 1861-1865--Personal narratives, Confederate. | Ely, Martha Frances, 1834-1924--Correspondence. | Soldiers--Georgia--Correspondence. | Ely family.
Classification: LCC E559.5 54th .E49 2016 | DDC 973.7/459092--dc23
LC record available at http://lccn.loc.gov/2016009372

Contents

Preface

Some thirty years ago my father's uncle appeared at his back door and told him he was too old to live alone and needed a place to live out his last days. James Blakeley was ninety years old and my parents graciously invited him to move in. Uncle Jim was a bachelor and a very intelligent old gentleman. My children fell in love with him and he became very fond of them.

As he approached his hundredth birthday (still living in my parents' home), Uncle Jim asked my father to clean out his home in Woodbury, Georgia and sell it for him. He told my father that he wanted to give my daughter his grandparents' bedroom suite; he mentioned that after his grandmother's death in 1924, the family had closed her bedroom door and had not disturbed it. My father went to pick up the bedroom suite, turned over the mattresses on the bed, and discovered a large yellowed pillowcase filled with papers and a small book. Daddy brought the bedroom suite and the pillowcase back to Columbus.

Later that evening, I received a phone call from my father asking me to come over. When I got there, my Uncle Jim said to me, "You are the family historian and you should have these papers that belonged to my grandmother." I thanked him for his generosity, thinking to myself, my daughter gets the bedroom suite and I get an old pillowcase!

I took the pillowcase home, sat down on the floor of my living room, and began to pull out letters written by my great-great-grandfather during the Civil War along with other letters from the family. As I looked through the pillowcase, I found more than 130 letters Marcus Bethune Ely had written to his beloved wife during the Civil War. Along with the letters from Marcus, there were a few letters from Mattie (his wife) and the Bible Marcus carried during the war. I would love to say I started transcribing the letters immediately, but I can't. My husband constantly encouraged me to begin the project, but it wasn't until 2010 that I decided to transcribe the letters.

At first, I only wanted to transcribe the letters and publish them. As I read the letters I began to have questions about the men in the unit he wrote about and the places his unit found themselves in. I am a very curious person and I found myself poring through reels of newspaper microfilm, looking at census records, writing countless letters, collecting wills and other documents, e-mailing countless people through my research efforts on ancestry.com, looking at records of the unit at Fold3.com, typing in the name of every man in the unit at findagrave.com, and searching through endless books and manuscripts at the Georgia Archives and the Columbus Public Library. I have visited the Beaulieu area in Savannah, Georgia; Hardeeville, South Carolina; Purrysburg, South Carolina; Ft. Gaines, Georgia; and all the battle sites in the Atlanta area and north Georgia and so many of the men's graves. I haven't found all the answers to questions that I have about this family, their neighbors, and the sad time they endured, but it has given me a greater insight into my ancestors and their willingness to suffer great hardships for a cause they believed in.

—Linda McCardle

Acknowledgments

Much gratitude goes to my husband, William McCardle, for prodding me to start this project and for accompanying me to forts in the Savannah area, courthouses, cemeteries, and battlefield sites in Georgia and Alabama. Thank you, dear family, for your encouragement and understanding my need to visit just "one more cemetery." Many thanks go to Callie B. McGinnis, retired Dean of Libraries at Columbus State University and experienced genealogist, for her willingness to provide feedback; and Kathy Gierer, retired MCSD educator, Advisor College of Education and Health Professions, Columbus State University, and contributor to *Columbus Ledger-Enquirer*, for her outstanding editing skills. I also want to thank Louise Calhoun Barfield, the author of *The History of Harris County, 1827–1961,* for the years of research she put into her book. Though she's no longer with us, this book has been an invaluable resource to me and countless others searching for their ancestors.

Introduction

On Sunday morning May 15, 1864, 2nd Lieutenant Marcus Ely and the 54th Georgia Regiment were in line of battle west of Calhoun, Georgia, facing three huge divisions of Sherman's army intent on capturing Atlanta and bringing the South to its knees. Though Marcus Ely's unit, the Russell Guards, had been in the war for two years, they had not experienced any major battles. They were ordered to Dalton, Georgia on April 24, 1864 and arrived in Dalton on May 2. Immediately they were involved in the opening battles of the Atlanta Campaign. In an abbreviated letter Marcus scrawled May 7 ordered to the front, May 8 in line of battle near Rocky Face Ridge. He wrote the following words in his Bible:

> Sunday morning May 15th 64 West of Calhoun, Ga
> "If I fall in this battle, I lose my life in a just and holy cause and I know you will cherish my memory in your heart." MBEly

Marcus Ely was an educated man; before the war he had been a teacher. He was apparently a religious man, as he often stated that he was reading his Bible. He was a loving father, son, and husband. He wrote several times asking his wife to give his love to his father's slaves. The few surviving letters from his wife Mattie also contain comments about their slaves. They were concerned about their health and treatment, but thought nothing of selling them or hiring them out. In many of his letters, he stated that they were all making sacrifices so the South could be "free."

Reading Marcus and Mattie's words 150 years later, their thought processes are baffling. But, the letters that came into my possession are precious to me; they shed light on a family and a community struggling to survive hardship and heartache. They are a window into the daily life of a soldier on the Georgia coast and later in north Georgia. They record captures and deaths of soldiers, a heartbreaking love story, but most importantly survival. They offer us a realistic view of the South during the Civil War, particularly an affluent family with its roots firmly in Georgia soil.

The colony of Georgia was founded in 1733 by General James Oglethorpe, an English statesman, soldier, and philanthropist. Oglethorpe and a group of prominent Englishmen, concerned about the conditions of debtors' prisons and other social issues of the day, petitioned to establish a colony in Georgia.[1] Ironically, Georgia was set up to prevent it from becoming a colony of large plantations. No person could own more than 500 acres of land, and the original trustees were prevented from owning land or holding office in the colony.[2] In the original charter, slaves were forbidden. After Oglethorpe's final departure in 1743, slaves were allowed in the colony.

Between the founding of the colony and the Revolutionary War, Georgia's population swelled from 2,000 to more than 15,000.[3] In 1799, Jesse Ely (Marcus Ely's grandfather) moved into Greene County, Georgia. He purchased 235 acres of land for $400.[4] In 1817 he purchased an additional 500 acres for $1,500 on the south fork of the Little River.[5]

He married Nancy Haynes Shackleford, the widow of James Shackleford and the daughter of Parmenas Haynes. Parmenas Haynes was a captain in the Virginia Continental Line during the Revolutionary War.[6] Osborn Ely (the father of Marcus Ely) was Jesse's third son. As a young adult, Osborn was a teacher in a "poor school" in Greene County.[7] Poor schools were the forerunner of Georgia's public education system.

---

[1] Kenneth Coleman, *A History of Georgia* (Athens GA: University of Georgia Press, 1982) 16.

[2] Ibid., 17.

[3] Robert Famighetti, *1998 World Almanac and Book of Facts* (New York, NY: St. Martin's Press, 1997) 378.

[4] Freida R. Turner, *Greene County Georgia Land Records* (Macon GA: R.J. Taylor, Jr. Foundation, 1991) 216.

[5] Ibid., 104.

[6] Ettie Tidwell McCall, *Roster of Revolutionary Soldiers in Georgia*, 5 vols. (Baltimore MD: Genealogical Publishing Co., 1969) 3:109.

[7] Thaddeus B. Rice, *History of Greene County, Georgia 1786–1886* (Macon GA: J. W. Burke & Co., 1961) 210.

The poor schools gave the children of factory, farm, and other manual laborers an opportunity for a basic education.[8]

Osborn and Adjaline Birdsong were married in Oglethorpe County, Georgia on February 25, 1828.[9] They welcomed their first child, Ann, in 1830, followed by Marcus in 1831.[10] The young family along with several of Osborn's brothers attended Bethesda Baptist Church under the leadership of Reverend Jesse Mercer.[11] Mercer Institute, later Mercer University, founded in Penfield, Georgia, was named for Jesse Mercer. He was the first chair of the Board of Trustees.[12]

Osborn along with his brothers, Seaborn and Wellborn, moved into the frontier town of Columbus, Georgia in the 1830s. Columbus, established in 1828, quickly became a bustling town. Schools, churches, stores, and a theater were appearing soon. Mirabeau B. Lamar established the city's first newspaper, the *Columbus Enquirer*.[13]

In the period leading up to the Civil War, Columbus rapidly developed into a regional manufacturing and trading center, due in large part to its proximity to the Chattahoochee River.

Osborn, Adjaline, and their three small children settled in the eastern part of Muscogee County, Georgia. They became members of Bethel Baptist Church and Osborn served as recording secretary for several years.[14] Osborn also served on the Columbus School Board in 1839.[15]

---

[8] Ibid., 209.

[9] *Oglethorpe County, GA Marriages*, Book A, 119.

[10] *1840 U.S. Federal Census*, Muscogee County, District 744, 322.

[11] Vivian Cates, *Conference Minutes of Bethesda Baptist Church, Union Point, Greene County, GA August 1817 to December 1865*, 51, 55, 59.

[12] Charles Jones, *Education in Georgia* (Washington DC: U.S. Government Printing Office, 1889) 61.

[13] Etta Blanchard Worsley, *Columbus on the Chattahoochee* (Columbus GA: Columbus Printing Co., 1951) 66.

[14] *Bethel Baptist Church Minutes, Columbus, GA. 1829–1872.*

[15] Nancy Telfair, *A History of Columbus, GA 1828–1928* (Columbus GA: Historical Publishing Co., 1929) 100.

In the early 1840s, Osborn bought two farms in Randolph County while remaining in Columbus.[16] An ad ran in the Columbus newspaper in 1843, stating that a runaway slave, Sam, had been seen in the vicinity of Osborn Ely's farm. Sam's wife, also a slave, was working on the farm in Ft. Gaines.[17] While visiting Fort Gaines in 1843, Adjaline died.[18] On August 18, 1844, Osborn married Jane Russell, the daughter of William and Mary Russell.[19]

In 1848, Osborn bought 800 acres of land in Harris County about fifteen miles from Columbus.[20] The 1850 Slave Schedule reported that Osborn Ely owned twenty-four slaves.[21] The Ely family moved their membership to Rehobeth Baptist Church in Cataula, Georgia and settled into the community.[22]

Marcus attended the Brownwood Institute in LaGrange, Georgia, graduating in 1850 with a teaching degree.[23] In 1837, Brownwood Institute was founded by Dr. Robert C. Brown. It was originally a girls' school. After his death, Brownwood passed through several owners before the Rev. Otis Smith, a Baptist minister, made it a male university. Brownwood closed during the War Between the States, never to successfully reopen.[24]

The 1850s had been prosperous for the Ely family. By 1860 Osborn Ely had increased his family to twelve children, his slaves to

---

[16] *Randolph County, Georgia, Deed Book F*, 178, 199.

[17] "Runaway Slave," *The Columbus* (GA) *Enquirer*, 7 June 1843.

[18] Mary McKeown Overly, *Obituaries Published in the Christian Index* (Macon GA: Georgia Baptist Historical Society, Mercer University Press, 1975) 70.

[19] *Muscogee County, GA, Record of Marriages, Book A, 1838–1845*, 246.

[20] *Harris County, GA Deed Book H*, 128; *Deed Book O*, 23; *Deed Book P*, 139.

[21] *1850 U.S. Federal Census, Slave Schedule*, Georgia, Harris County, 435.

[22] Louise Calhoun Barfield, *History of Harris County, GA, 1827–1961* (LaGrange GA: Cherith Creek Designs, 1961) 368.

[23] From private papers of Martha Frances Ely, in possession of editor. ("Marcus Bethune Ely completed his education at Brownwood Institute in 1850. Chose teaching as his profession, which profession he adored. Taught in many sections of his own state and also in Alabama.")

[24] Clifford Lewis Smith, *History of Troup Co., GA* (Atlanta GA: Foote and Davies, 1935) 134.

thirty-seven,[25] and his personal wealth to $36,400 and land value to $4,000.[26] (In today's economy Osborn's worth would be well over a million dollars.)[27]

Marcus met Martha Frances "Mattie" Dumas in LaGrange where she was attending the LaGrange Female College.[28] LaGrange College began as a female academy. At that time, educational institutions in Georgia were not allowed to grant degrees to women so the term "academy" indicated that subjects being taught, such as mathematics and science, were over and above finishing schools. In 1843, Joseph and Hugh Montgomery bought the academy. After receiving a charter to give college degrees to women, the academy's name was changed to LaGrange Female Institute in 1847, to LaGrange Female College in 1851, and to LaGrange College in 1934.[29]

Mattie was the daughter of Moses Dumas and Frances Hendley. The Dumases were a prosperous middle-class family. The Dumas family migrated from North Carolina into Monroe County, Georgia in the 1830s.[30] They were also slave owners. In the 1860 Federal Slave Schedule, Moses Dumas reported eight slaves.[31]

Marcus and Mattie married in 1855 in Mattie's hometown of Barnesville.[32] They moved to Fort Gaines, Georgia, an outpost on the Chattahoochee River where Marcus taught school.[33] During their time in

---

[25] *1860 U.S. Federal Census, Slave Schedule, Georgia, Harris County, Georgia, 707 Georgia Militia District 707*, 77.

[26] *1860 U.S. Federal Census, Georgia, Harris County, 707 Georgia Militia District*, 64.

[27] "Purchasing Power of Money in the United States from 1774 to Present," Ssamuel. Williamson, last modified 2015, http://www.measuring worth.com.

[28] From private papers of Martha Frances Ely, in possession of editor. ("Finished her education at LaGrange Female College in eighteen hundred and fifty three.")

[29] Smith, *History of Troup Co.*, 139.

[30] *1840 U.S. Federal Census, Georgia, Monroe County, District 504*, 15.

[31] *1850 U.S. Federal Census, Slave Schedule, Georgia, Monroe County*, 459.

[32] "Married," *Columbus* (GA) *Enquirer*, 8 May 1855, 3.

[33] *1860 U.S. Federal Census, Georgia, Clay County, District 49*, 29.

Fort Gaines Marcus and Mattie began their family. Elizabeth "Lizzie" Birdsong was born in 1856 and Edwin Dumas arrived in 1859.[34]

Columbus and the surrounding area grew rapidly during the years preceding the Civil War, cotton being the catalyst for the growth. In 1851 the railroad line reached Columbus, allowing both rail and river transportation.[35] In 1860, Columbus was a prosperous city boasting gristmills, textile mills, and other small industrial operations. The election of Abraham Lincoln brought the differences between the North and South to a head, resulting in the secession of South Carolina on December 20, 1860.[36] Georgia seceded from the Union on January 19, 1861.[37]

The citizens of Columbus and surrounding areas immediately formed military units and the women formed aid societies to furnish clothing and other articles of comfort for husbands, fathers, and brothers.[38] The ladies of Cataula organized the Cataula Ladies Aid Society. This group collected socks, drawers, gloves, and other materials for the soldiers. They solicited aid from prominent Harris County citizens. Mrs. T. F. Brewster, Carrie Minter, Mrs. McLeroy, Mrs. Osborn Ely, and Lucy and Sallie Ely were just a few of the members of the group.[39]

Columbus quickly turned its civilian operations to the war effort. Columbus became a manufacturer of military clothing and other needed textiles. Wagon factories sprang up and the Columbus Iron Works produced artillery pieces, cannons, and mortars.[40] Columbus was home to the largest shoe factory in the South during the years of conflict. There was also a sword factory that produced swords, bayonets, and pistols. But

---

[34] *Ely Family Bible Records, 1873.*

[35] Worsley, *Columbus on the Chattahoochee,* 183.

[36] Walter B. Edgar, *South Carolina: A History* (Columbia SC: University of South Carolina Press, 1998) 352.

[37] Coleman, *A History of Georgia,* 188.

[38] Worsley, *Columbus on the Chattahoochee,* 283.

[39] Barfield, *History of Harris County,* 293.

[40] Worsley, *Columbus on the Chattahoochee,* 285.

Columbus's most significant contribution by far was the production of steam engines and boilers for gunboats.[41]

Marcus and Mattie returned to the Columbus area between 1860 and 1861. Marcus and three of his brothers decided to enlist in the Russell Guards, formed by Marcus's stepuncle Charles Russell in May 1862. The unit was a mixture of Muscogee and Harris County citizens. By 1862 there were more than two dozen military units from Muscogee County and surrounding areas. Units were sent north and east.[42]

Marcus and the Russell Guards arrived in the Savannah area by the middle of May 1862. The Russell Guards were in the Savannah area until February 1864. The company moved to the Hardeeville, South Carolina area toward the end of February. Marcus spent a lot of time on picket duty guarding the Savannah River Trestle. The years the Russell Guards spent in Savannah were relatively uneventful for their unit; however, Marcus's letters contain a great deal of information about events in the Savannah and Charleston areas. On May 2, 1862 the Russell Guards arrived by train in Dalton and found themselves facing Sherman's forces and the beginning of the Atlanta Campaign. The unit was involved in the battles around Resaca, Dalton, Rocky Face Ridge, Calhoun, Kennesaw Mountain, and Jonesboro, Georgia, as well as Murfreesboro and Franklin, Tennessee, Meridian, Mississippi, and Bentonville, North Carolina. They surrendered at Greensboro, North Carolina on April 25, 1865.[43] Through the letters of Marcus and Mattie, the despair, loneliness, and suffering of the soldiers and their families are vividly portrayed. More importantly, the letters reflect the love and hope that survived the most tragic time in our country's history.

---

[41] John S. Lupold, *Columbus, Georgia 1828–1878* (Columbus GA: Columbus Sesquicentennial, Inc., 1978) 33.

[42] Worsley, *Columbus on the Chattahoochee,* 283.

[43] Lillian Henderson, ed., *Roster of the Confederate Soldiers of Georgia*, 6 vols. (Hapeville GA: Longino and Porter, Inc., 1960) 5:699.

Marcus Bethune Ely was born in 1831. He attended Brownwood Institute (LaGrange, Georgia) in the early 1850s. Before the war he taught school in Fort Gaines, Georgia. This photo was probably taken before 1860.

After the war, Marcus Bethune Ely farmed for a short time but eventually returned to teaching. He taught in the Columbus, Georgia, area and started several schools in the Lee County, Alabama, area. Marcus was named Principal of the Browneville Public School in 1878 and briefly served as Superintendent in the Girard Public School System (Phenix City, Alabama). Marcus Bethune Ely died in Columbus, Georgia, at his home on Troop Street April 5, 1880.

Martha Frances (Mattie) Dumas Ely was born in 1834. She attended LaGrange Female College in LaGrange, Georgia. She and Marcus married in Barnesville, Georgia, on May 1, 1855. After the war, Mattie and Marcus taught school in Georgia and Alabama. After Marcus's death, Mattie and her daughter Elizabeth Birdsong Ely continued to teach in the Browneville, Alabama, (Lee County) area.

Elizabeth Birdsong Ely Blakeley, the eldest child of Marcus and Mattie Ely, was born in 1856. She is mentioned as "Sister" numerous times in Marcus and Mattie's letters. She married Abram Blakeley in 1878 and continued to teach with her mother after Marcus's death.

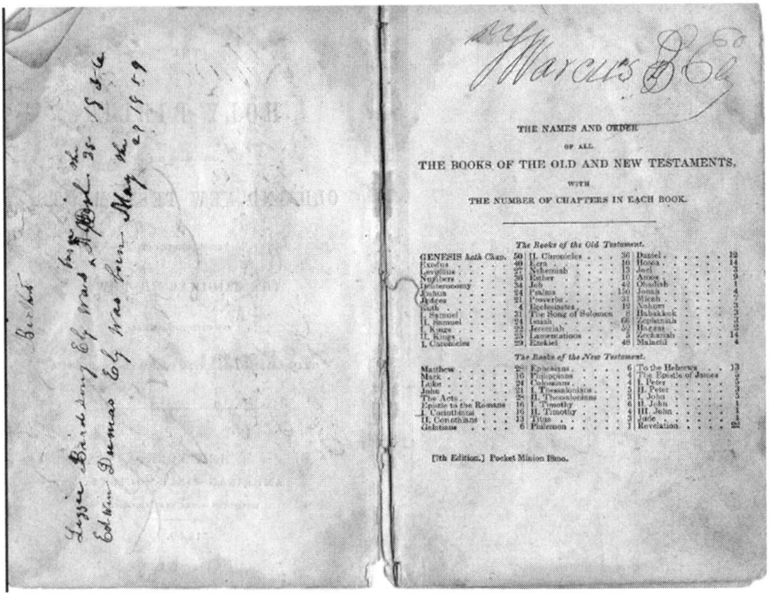

A front page of the small bible Marcus Ely carried during his time in the Russell Guards (Co. H, 54th Georgia Infantry). The birth dates of his first two children are recorded on the page adjacent to the table of contents.

Marcus Bethune Ely, along with two of his children (Lucy Osborn and Edwin Dumas Ely), is buried in historic Linwood Cemetery in Columbus, Georgia.

Map of Georgia, ca 1860, showing battle sites, rivers, and railroad lines mentioned in letters of Marcus and Mattie Ely.

1862

"I Fear I Don't Get Half Your Letters"

An advertisement was placed in the Columbus Daily Enquirer on April 29, 1862 by Captain Charles R. Russell. The article stated he had been given authority to raise a company of not less than twenty men and to pay a $50 bounty and clothing money for recruitment. The advertisement also stated that when the company was raised and if the majority agreed, arrangements would be made to join Colonel Way's Regiment in Savannah. The advertisement instructed applicants to apply at Ingram & Russell's Law Office over Bedell & Co.'s store. By early May 1862, the Russell Guards had been formed and were on their way to Savannah.[1]

Camp Way, near Savannah,

My Dear Wife

I mailed a letter to you yesterday, but as I have a chance of writing and sending another by Dr. B I write again. We are now at Camp Way[2]– 2 miles below Savannah – as nothing of special interest has transpired since date of my last – I must be brief this time. This regiment is now organized – We have a very fine looking set of men. I am as well satisfied as I could reasonably expect. Of course my thoughts for the most part are directed homeward but I live in the hope of a joyful reunion - "How blessing brightens as they take their flight." Nathan McLeroy[3] is sick with the mumps. Bass[4] is also unwell. My company is not yet organized,

---

[1] "Company Wanted," *Columbus* (GA) *Daily Enquirer*, 29 April 1862, 2.

[2] The 54th Regiment camped from May 15, 1862–June 28, 1862 on White Bluff Road in Chatham County, Georgia. Wm. S. Smedlund, *Campfires of GA Troops, 1861-1865* (Kennesaw Mountain Press) 286.

[3] Nathan McLeroy was a private in the Russell Guards and a neighbor of the Ely family. Henderson, *Roster of the Confederate Soldiers*, 5:705.

[4] Bass (Mr. Bass) is mentioned quite often and Marcus speaks of him trying to get a discharge, but he is not listed in the records of the Russell Guards.

only that Dr. Brewster[5] is 1st Lieutenant. My prospects for 2nd Lieutenant are cheeringly bright. Some rumors this morning that the Yanks will attack Savannah soon. My health is very good indeed – am getting that nervous weakness. Love & kiss my children. I'll write to you soon. Yours forever, MBE

Camp Way, near Savannah, May 22, 1862

My Dearest Mattie,

As I have written very often since I left home I shall only give you a half sheet this time I have not heard a syllable from you yet. When you write my dear you must not wait for an answer but keep writing as the presumption is I shall not get all your letters. I will again give you the proper directions for fear that I did not do so properly in my last direct Marcus B Ely Co. H 54 Reg. GA Vol Savannah, GA – I suppose you have received a letter I wrote some days since in which I stated to you the position I occupied salary &c. If you did not get the letter in which I gave you all these particulars let me know and I'll write them again. Jimmy[6] and I went fishing on the Savannah – Jimmy hung a very large fish which broke his line I did not catch anything. I shall not fish much as I am afraid to go down on the river. There is so much decayed vegetable matter I might take the fever. I am very particular. I bathe as often as I can and keep my clothes as clean as possible. Without these precautions it is almost impossible for a soldier to be healthy in camp. We have been compelled to eat half cooked victuals for some time. We could not get cooking utensils in Savannah and the government does not furnish them. We were obliged to buy a cooking stove. You ought to see me cooking on it. We have 14 in our mess and the stove cost us a dollar

---

[5] Dr. Tomlinson Fort Brewster was a physician in Harris County, also a neighbor of the Ely family and a member of the Russell Guards (see Co. H 54th "The Russell Guards" Biographies). Barfield, *History of Harris County*, 382.

[6] Jimmy was the brother of Marcus Ely (see Ely and Dumas Family Biographies). Ibid., 384.

each. As soon as the officers get fixed up I shall tent and mess with them. My love you must try to be contented. I shall come home to see you and the children often. Kiss them for me. God bless their souls. Tell them Pa will bring some nice things when he comes. When you write tell me what my boy says about his Pa's being gone to the war – Be cheerful and contented and believe me as ever.

Your devoted husband MBE

Camp Way, near Savannah, May 28, 1862

My Dear Wife,

I had the pleasure of receiving the box, bundle & letter you had the kindness to send me by Lieut. T.F. Brewster. I prized all, but the letter received the warmest greeting. It was the first and only letter that I have received from you and of course I was getting somewhat uneasy. I hope my dear you will write as often as you can, as I would cheerfully walk ten miles every day to get a letter from you. I shall write to you two or three times a week & I should be glad for you to write as often, if you can. You must not expect to get a connected or systematic letter from me at any time. My tent is generally crowded with men talking, laughing, singing &c In addition to this "May be" if I get a good start I'll keep trotting till I get home. Some of our boys are the most homesick fellows you ever read of. They do not act like men, but like a sick kitten whining about, - a small number of them are in this condition – the rest are very well contented. My dear I can find present use for everything you have sent me. You are well aware that I am the boy to dispose of the eggs. As to the butter that will not be in my way long- as well as the other provisions. I got mad in Columbus & would not have the government furnished to our Company. They were almost as coarse as gunny bagging I have had not others except my old blacks – which I have mended several times and kept them together. The jacket is very nice. Some of the officers wanted it but it could not be had for love or money. In a word I heartily thank you my dear for your kindness and forethought. I get my washing done at about fifty cents per month.

This camp is the "dirtiest" place you ever saw. If I should change my clothing every day I could not keep neat I take plenty of exercise – wash my arms neck and feet everyday & take a general bath twice a week. Then as I have no guard or drill duty to do I hope I shall remain healthy. I believe I am quite well at present, only I have a boil under my left arm which pains me exceedingly I shall take a "dose" of salts one of these mornings. The health of our company is presently good. We have had but one man in the Hospital (Nathan McLeroy) and he has recovered and returned to camp. A few of our boys are complaining but none of them seriously sick. My dear I shall try to get a furlough about the 8th or 9th of June. Capt. Russell[7] will be at home in a day or two& will let me have a furlough if I apply for it. You must not leave home until I come as I wish to take you out to Monroe. I wish I could see you & my little darlings. Give my love to Pa & Ma sister and all the family. I'll write again in a few days and let you know what day to expect me I suppose Bro James will come with me or he may come before. Tell Mandy Anderson is well – Remember me to all Pa's "niggers."[8]

Write soon to your loving husband MBEly

Camp Way, near Savannah, May 31, 1862

My Dearest Mattie,

Your very welcomed letter sent by Mr. Bass was received & you may be rest assured I was glad to hear from you. I had just written to you & given all the ideas of interest, but as I expected to go to Savannah this morning I could not forbear scratching you a few lines. I have reason to

---

[7] Charles Rienzi Russell[7] formed the Russell Guards in 1862. He was the brother of Jane Russell Ely, Osborn's second wife. Pa and Ma were Osborn and Jane Russell Ely (see Co. H 54th "The Russell Guards" Biographies).

[8] The 1860 Slave Schedule reported that Osborn Ely owned thirty-seven slaves and Marcus Ely owned two slaves.[8] Mandy and Anderson were not able to be identified. 1850 U.S. Federal Census, Georgia, Muscogee County, 9th District, 767.

be thankful that you are all enjoying good health and I have the happiness to inform you that I am quite well both as to mind and body. The health of our company is very good. We have no serious case of sickness and those who are complaining are generally on hand about meal time.

My dear you spoke of hiring Mary[9] to cousin Nancy Birdsong[10] I am perfectly willing to that arrangement. You wrote that a Mr. Roberson from Andrews Company passed up the wall. You were mistaken Mr R was from Murphy's Company. His corpse passed our camp. Capt Russell has not returned yet. We look for him on the morning's train. I shall try to get a furlough to start on the 9th of June. The Military Laws are very stringent, however I do not think I will have any difficult in getting off. If so I'll inform you. My principal object in coming home is to take you to Monroe – so you must not leave before you hear from me again. If there are any other stringent laws made preventing the granting of furloughs I shall make arrangements for you & the children to come to Savannah to see me for I am determined to see you occasionally at all events thats certain. Mr. Bass says tell his wife he is well – also that his chances to get a discharge are very good. The surgeon told him yesterday that his chances to get a discharge are very good. He said to tell his wife to make "Dave _____" and feed the pigs &c. If Mr. B leaves in a few days I'll write by him, shall write to sister also. Say to Mrs. Brawner that Lem[11] is well and in good spirits – also that he is like cold souse always ready for duty & gets that praise from all the officers. All of our

---

[9] National Archives, Compiled Service Records of Confederate Soldiers from Georgia Units, Catalog ID 586957, Record Group 109, 54th Infantry, Marcus B. Ely, 1863. Mary was the property of Marcus and Mattie Ely (her story is found in People and Places).

[10] Nancy Hawkins Birdsong was the wife of Edward Birdsong, Marcus Ely's cousin. *1850 U.S. Federal Census, Georgia, Muscogee County*, 668.

[11] James Lemuel Brawner ("Lem") was a resident of Harris County and a private in the Russell Guards. Henderson, *Roster of the Confederate Soldiers*, 5:701.

neighborhood boys are well. Bro. Jimmy is as fat as a pig – He will be at home probably in a few days.

Kiss the children. Love to all Write soon to your affectionate Husband MBE

Camp Way, near Savannah, June 1, 1862

My dear wife,

It is with the greatest pleasure on this beautiful Sabbath morning that I pen you a brief note. I received your kind letter by Captain Russell and although I had just mailed a letter to you, I write again by Mr. Bass as you will doubtless get this before you get the one through the mail. Brother James is at present undecided whether he will go on with Mr. Bass or remain a few days longer. I will send letters by him. As to Bro. J's being "mustered into service" that is altogether a mistake. When he comes home he will stay if he does not get the sutler's[12] position. I can not imagine who put out that report. My dear, I do not want you by any means to leave before I get back. Of course, I expect to go with you to Monroe. I do not think it proper for you to take that trip by yourself. I presume it is unnecessary to say anything about any of the boys as most of them will send letters by Bass. My dear, as Bass is on the eve of leaving I am compelled to be brief. Do you need any money? Let me know when you write so that I may know what to draw when I start home. You ask if my pants fit, I find no objection to them in the world. My jacket is too small & the sleeves too short, but I suppose you cut it according to your cloth. It does very well when I wear my coat & I cut all sorts of a fancy figure- expect to wear it in church this morning. We have singings in camp every night & some of the companies prayer meetings is held. I frequently attend the prayer meetings. There are several Baptist preachers in the regiment. There is a great deal of profanity in the

[12] A sutler was a merchant that followed military units selling foods and other goods. Michael O. Varhola, *Life in Civil War America* (Cincinnati OH: Family Tree Books, 2011) 227.

regiment – but I am pleased to say – very little in our company. Orders have been read at the separate parades to punish all who are guilty of profanity and since there has been a great change for the better. My dear, I write so frequently that I got out of "soap." Of course you know it will be the happiness of my existence when I again meet you and our precious children. I am well & cheerful and look forward to pleasure to our meeting which will be the 10th inst [in the same month] if I am not disappointed.

Your loving husband, MBE

Savannah, June 23, 1862

My Dear Wife,

As I am aware you are anxious to hear from me, I take the earliest opportunity of dropping you a line. I arrived at Camp Way yesterday "right side up with care." I was quite feeble on Saturday the day I left Barnesville but since yesterday I am happy to inform you that my health is gradually improving. Quite a number of our company along with Lt. Bedell[13] are in the hospital. I am sorry to say the general health of our company and regiment is not as good as could be desired. My dear, I have applied for regiment clerk[14] and I think my chances for getting the situation quite flattering. If I succeed it will increase my monthly pay to nearly 100.00. My love, I am uneasy about our children. I trust however they are well. I desire you write as soon as possible to let me know. Mrs. Brewster has followed the Dr. She is lodging at a private home in the city. Of course, Lieutenant Dr. Brewster is immensely delighted, who

---

[13] Henderson, *Roster of the Confederate Soldiers,* 5:699. Lieutenant John K. Bedell was in the Russell Guards (see Co. H 54th "The Russell Guards" Biographies).

[14] The regiment, or company, clerk was responsible for maintaining the paperwork for the regiment. "Military Structure," Roots Web, last modified 2003, http://www.rootsweb.ancestry.com/mnwabcw.31.htm.

would not be under similar circumstances? Bob[15] has typhoid fever[16] and is at the same house with his sister. Brother J is well, he does not speak of going home. The conscript officer[17] came around but did not enroll him. Capt. Russell told him of his condition – physical disability and he seemed satisfied. You must excuse a short note this time. I'll give you a more extensive epistle hereafter.

Write soon to your True and Devoted Husband, Marcus B Ely

P.S. My love to Bro. William & family[18] also Sis Synthy[19] and all friends and relatives.

Savannah, June 28, 1862

My dear Beloved Mattie,

Your very kind letter of the 25th was received yesterday and I have hastened this morning to respond. I was extremely anxious about the children and the welcome intelligence of the restoration of their health lifted a load from my heart. I was extremely mortified to hear of your indisposition. But I sincerely hope that the next letter will bring the same cheering news in regard to your precious self. I believe my love that if at all times I could be assured of the health and prosperity of my friends and family nothing would ever daunt my spirit or disturb my happiness.

---

[15] Bob, or Robert Beall, was the brother of Margaret Beal Brewster. He served in the Russell Guards. Henderson, *Roster of the Confederate Soldiers,* 5:701.

[16] Typhoid fever was an infectious disease characterized by high fevers and intestinal bleeding. It was spread through the camps during the Civil War due to unsanitary conditions. Glenna Schroeder-Lein, *The Encyclopedia of Civil War Medicine* (Armonk NY: M.E. Sharpe, Inc., 2008) 310.

[17] The conscript officer was a person employed by the military to recruit soldiers for the army. Coleman, *A History of Georgia,* 189.

[18] William Watson married Elizabeth Dumas, Mattie's older sister. The Watson family lived in Barnesville, Georgia. *1850 U.S. Federal Census, Georgia, Monroe County,* 68.

[19] Synthia "Synthy" Dumas was also Mattie's older sister.*Dumas Family Bible Records,* 1824.

It is true to be separated from my dear loved ones is a bitter pill but I bear it *cheerfully* for my bleeding country's sake. Yes and by the help of our great God we will beat back the insolent foe from our Southern soil and establish the independence guaranteed to us by our Revolutionary forefathers. Nothing short of this will satisfy a true patriot. May God Almighty speed the day when peace shall be established & that each soldier may return to his family to enjoy liberty the price of blood. My love I was deeply deeply mortified to hear of the death of Jerry's[20] wife poor fellow. How very sad must be his heart. Write to him and assure him of my affection and sympathy. You spoke of going down to your fathers. Remember me affectionately to him and in fact to all friends and relatives. My love, I am not in want of any clothing. But the box you spoke of will not come amiss. When you need money let me know and you shall have it. No news about Savannah except that several English vessels have run the blockade and brought in arms and many other things. I learned that one was filled with fruit. If so, I will send you a box of oranges and bannahas — My love we have just heard of the great victory in Virginia I hope it is all true. Will write again soon I shall know this morning if I got the position on the non-commissioned staff I spoke of last. Write soon my love and write often. Remember after the first of July my love you must pay 10 cents on letters.

Your Devoted Husband, MBEly

Savannah, GA June 30th 1862

My dearest Mattie,

I address you a few lines this morning as I have not written to you in two or three days. Besides, I shall not have the privilege after today of the old postage rates but that is nothing of much misfortune for if letter postage should be doubled once a month I should write no less letters to you. We are all in a stir this morning. General inspection drill will come off in a few minutes and the boys are very busily engaged cleaning up

[20] Jerry Dumas was Mattie's youngest brother. (The story of Jerry and Jeanette Iola Pope Dumas is told in Ely and Dumas Family Biographies.)

their guns. We will be paid off in a few days, if you want any money let me know. I shall send between 50 & 100 dollars home to Pa. We have received glorious news from Richmond. Would that old McClellan[21] and his grand army were totally routed and exterminated and that the olive branch of peace shall be brought into our border. We had a false alarm the other night. The long roll[22] was beat and all over the encampment was heard the cry – fall in men with knapsacks and accoutrements. It was about midnight. We started double quick and formed the battle line beyond our encampment. Some of the boys stumbled over a wood pile and fell. Some of the boys in the excitement lost their companies and were running around "Where is Company C? Where is Company H? &c." The alarm was given to accustom us to falling in promptly. My love I have received the position of Reg. Clerk though it does not increase my pay much it is a very nice place. It brings me in contact with the Staff Officers and I am allowed many liberties &c. I must close for the present. Write soon to your affectionate husband. MBEly

My love I close for want of more time. Remember me to relatives & friends.

---

[21] Old McClellan was George B. McClellan, a Union General most famous for developing a calvary saddle aptly named the "McClellan Saddle." Henry E. Simmons, *A Concise Encyclopedia of the Civil War*(New York:NY:A.S. Barnes and Company, 1965)145.

[22] The long roll was a long snare drum roll to wake up or alert soldiers for action. John Wright, *The Language of the Civil War*, (Westport, CT: Oryx Press, 2001) 181.

Camp Way, near Savannah, July 5, 1862

My dearest,

Your very welcomed letter was received a day or two ago – I should have responded immediately, but for pressing duties. I have received the opportunity of Regimental Clerk and of course my time is not at my disposal. I shall however, have more leisure as soon as our adjutant gets well. My salary is now $71.00 per month and I am well pleased with my position and my love I was most happy to learn that you and the children have recovered your usual health. I know if you keep well, you will do well for you are among friends and that is a source of infinite satisfaction. Say to Bro Wm Dumas[23] that I do not think hard of him in the least and that I ever retain for him the warmest regard and affection. Also say to Sis Matt that I have never "taken any exceptions" and that I was never treated better anywhere in my life than at her house. My love you wrote that you dreamed that you were at Mrs. Brewster's boarding house with me. I trust my love that you will realize that dream ere the expiration of many weeks. And I sincerely hope that the war will soon close _that there may be many many happy reunions & none more happy than ours. Before I get it I will tell you that Mrs. Brewster has gone home. Of course Dr. Lt B got another furlough & went too – also Robert Beall on sick furlough. My love Bro J received a letter from Sister yesterday The white family are well_ The negroes have been very sick _ at least a large number of them Marsh's wife Zoo is dead__ Carrie Minter[24] was married a short time ago to a man from Ala. My love I shall go to Savannah today If there is any fruit there I shall send you a box in a few days. I shall also send you some money soon. I shall draw my money in a

---

[23] William Henley Dumas, the brother of Mattie Ely, married Martha "Matt" Ann Kendrick. They lived in Zebulon, GA (Pike County). Lavinia Zellner Horne, *History, Biography, and Genealogy of the Dumas-Morris Families.* (Georgia Archives Despository, Atlanda, GA: LCZ Horne Publications) 12–13.

[24] Carrie Minter married William James Saxon, a school teacher from Loachapoka, Alabama. William Saxon joined the Loachapocha Rifles and was wounded. After the war the family settled in Lee County, AL, where William continued to teach school until his death. Barfield, *History of Harris County,* 74.

short time and shall send it to you or Pa as the risk is too great to keep it in the camp I forgot to tell you there has been rain in Harris and prospect (July) good for more I wrote to cousin Nancy Birdsong's folks not long since & requested them to give my pipe to Pa &c. I am sorry Jerry did not pass through Barnesville while I was there as I was anxious to see him. My dear there was an election this morning for junior 2nd Lieut in our company & William Hightower[25] was elected. There was a great deal of contention & hard feeling among the men I took no part in it—did not vote—was not a candidate. I would not change my position for nothing less than Brig. Gen for I have no guard or fatigue duty_ drill or nothing of the kind to do hence I have no cause to expose myself to the sun & diseaser of this unwholesome climate. We have quite a number on the sick list, but no very serious cases M.L. Brawner[26] is just creeping out of a spell of bilious fever.[27] Sandford Brannon[28] is quite sick with measles I am very sorry for the poor fellow. I wish he could get a discharge and go home to his family. The news from Richmond is highly interesting & satisfactory assurance that McClellan is badly cut off in fact most totally cut off [several lines unreadable] ...bring about a speedy peace My dear on yesterday (4th July) the Yankees had a tremendous "kick up" down at Ft. Pulaski[29] For 4 hours the booming of cannon was

---

[25] William Hightower was a member of the Russell Guards (see Co. H. 54th "The Russell Guards. (See Co. H 54th "Russell Guards" biographies.) Henderson, *Roster of the Confederate Soldiers,* 5:704

[26] M. L. Brawner was a resident of Harris County and a 3rd Sargeant in the Russell Guards. (See Co. H 54th "Russell Guards" biographies.) Barfield, *History of Harris County,* 545.

[27] Bilious fever was also called typhus fever, brain fever, spotted fever, and camp fever. It is also a term loosely applied to other intestinal and malarial fevers. Glenna Schroeder-Lien, Glenn, *The Encyclopedia of Civil War Medicine,* (Armonk, NY: M.E. Sharpe INC, 2008), 310.

[28] Sanford Brannon was the brother of Walter Brannon; there is no record of him enlisting in any unit during the Civil War. *1850 Federal Census, Georgia, Harris County, Crawford District,* 231.

[29] Fort Pulaski was constructed after the War of 1812 to protect the United States coasts from foreign invasions. The fort was completed in 1847. After

incessant… [not able to read] Letters from Judson & George state that they are well & anxious to get on their way & tell Lizzie & son to send a kiss for Pa. Remember me to all relatives and friends. My love I must close. I have done my best to write you ten cents worth as postage has doubled my dear you must double the length of your letters.

Write immediately to your very affectionate husband MBEly

I enclose a sample of cloth. If you can buy me a suit like it or similar to it I would be glad Let me know and I will try to make arrangements to send you any patterns &c Brother J has not joined our company I have persuaded him not to join but to go home & if the conscript gets him he will be exempted You must write to sister as she is anxious to hear from you and the children, if you can send me a few eatables such as butter eggs &c by express I can assure you they will be taken in according to

---

Camp Way, near Savannah, July 7, 1862

My dearest,

I have just finished perusing your very kind letter of 4th July. I am glad you are so punctual and I write immediately in reply so that you may not have any reason to complain of delay on my part. My dear instead of dating your letter July 4th it was dated June 4th but I know it was an oversight of yours and of course I care but little about the date so that I can hear from you often. My love I went down to Harrison's Regiment

---

South Carolina seceded from the Union, Governor Joe Brown ordered the fort to be taken by the state of Georgia. After Georgia seceded in 1861, Confederate troops moved into the fort. In late 1861, Union forces began moving onto Tybee Island after Confederate troops abandoned the area. On April 10, 1862 Union forces began a bombardment of Pulaski after asking Colonel Charles Olmstead, commander of the fort, to surrender. He refused, but after thirty hours of assault on the fort, Olmstead surrendered. The Union maintained control of the fort until the end of the war.Ralston B. Lattimore, *Fort Pulaski National Monument Georgia* (Washington DC: National Park Service Historical Handbook Series, No.16, 1954) 4–5.

(one mile below ours) and spent the day with Kelon & Jimmy Watson.[30] I was very glad to see the boys. Kelon was well, but his brother was quite feeble. He had been down with the measles and he looks quite thin and pale & is very anxious to get home on a furlough to recruit his health. Kelon had a nice dinner fixed up – plenty of chicken pie and fried eggs. The boys will spend next Sunday with me I shall try to get them up a good dinner to repay their kindness to me. Kelon speaks of writing to you soon. He and his brother are two as nice boys as any one would wish to see & I think when you see Kelon he will remind you very forcibly of Jerry Dumas. I forgot to tell you that I saw Sally Dumas on the train when I left Barnesville. She seemed very distant and of course I did not trouble myself to have many words with her. It is a little strange that none of James Dumas[31] children have been to see you. Of course I mean the girls. My love we have received glorious news this morning viz that the northern papers admit that their great general met with a terrible defeat near Richmond- also that England and France had declared their intention to put a stop to this war immediately. We have also received a disposition that old Lincoln has called out 300,000 and retaken the oath of allegiance and declared his intention of prosecuting the war to the bitter end. We have some bright hopes of peace God Send It for I would not give one hour of sweet enjoyment with my family for all the "pride, pomp and circumstance of war." I am willing to fight, but living in camp day after day and week after week is very tiresome. Sickness in camp about the same – some cases of chills and fever – hope my time will not come round. I think I have already had my full share – Wm. Hart[32] rec'd a letter from his brother Sam – Sam was wounded – Tom Moore was

---

[30] Kelon and Jimmy Watson were the sons of William and Synthia "Synthy" Watson. *1850 U.S. Federal Census, Georgia, Monroe County,* 136.

[31] Sally was Mattie's neice, the daughter of James Dumas. James Dumas was a very successful grocer in Forsyth, GA. *1860 U.S. Federal Census, Georgia, Monroe County*, 707.

[32] William Hart was a resident of Harris County, a neighbor of the Elys and a 4th Sergeant in the Russell Guards (see 54th Co. H "Russell Guards" biographies). Henderson, *Roster of the Confederate Soldiers,* 5:699.

killed –You remember he attended to Miss Walker's business last year. Almonds of Hamilton killed Askew, Mrs. Green's nephew was wounded. Remember me to all relatives. Tell Eddy and daughter to be good children. Brother J is well has not been mustered into service and speaks of going home soon.

Write my love to your most affectionate Husband MBEly

We will draw our pay soon & will send you as much as you want let me know if you are out of funds.

July 12, 1862

The enclosed letter was written yesterday but I failed to send it off. As I predicted I received your very dear letter I was of course most happy to receive your letter. My dear yesterday and last night I took some calomel[33] and quinine[34] and this morning some salts. I have taken it in order to try to ward off a threatened attack of bilious fever. Some of the boys will bring the box you spoke of from the express office. I haven't eat anything in two or three days but if you have sent some butter I can cut some. I will be well enough tomorrow to eat dinner with Kelon & Buddy at least I hope so. I am thankful for your kindness in sending the box. I hope to be well in a day or two. Write soon I want to hear from you.

Your affectionate husband MBE

---

[33] Calomel was a mercury-based medicine used to treat constipation as well as diarrhea. The overuse of calomel caused many soldiers to lose their teeth, and a number of soldiers died from mercury poisoning. Schroeder-Lein, *The Encyclopedia of Civil War Medicine,* 58.

[34] Quinine, derived from the bark of the South American cinchona tree, was used to treat malaria. A dose of "salts" was a form of Epsom salts also used to treat diarrhea. Joanna Hamilton Rajoppi, *New Brunswick and the Civil War* (Charleston SC: The History Press, 2013) 108.

Camp Way, near Savannah, July 24, 1862

My dearest Mattie

You perceive by "heading" of this letter that I have reached the camps and I take pleasure this morning in camp lying with my promise. My love I am in tolerable health – have not much reason to complain but still a little troubled with diarrhea – But as I have divided out all my fruit to the boys. I presume I will get well soon. I have not as yet returned to duty but shall do so this morning. My dear, Capt Russell asked why I did not stay longer and I am sorry that I did not remain a week longer for I returned to camp too soon that I want to see you and my little chaps just as bad as ever. My dear as I passed through Macon I saw Bro. James. He was going home, had just got up from an attack of fever – was looking badly. Rollen Russell[35] was with him – saw old Uncle Johnnie Thompson. The old man was well & looking about the same, He informed me that they have a flourishing school in the neighborhood. Crops pretty good. Rec'd a letter from Cousin Ret – she wrote but a few lines to ascertain where you were wanted to write to you. She says Uncle Billy McLeroy's family are sick as usual – the old gent having good spells and bad spells as is his custom. Ben & his company are at Chattanooga, TN. Visited the Watson boys yesterday. Jimmie is still feeble – does not seem to improve. They are coming up to see me this morning. L.M. Brawner is home on a ten day furlough sent a letter by him. The old fellow was powerful to get off. My love it is rumored that Dr. Lt. Brewster will resign - I can not say but I do not think he is satisfied. What do you think?—When I reached camp it was surrounded with armed men and cannon loaded with grape & canister shot. I was

---

[35] Rollen Russell was the younger brother of Charles R. Russell. He enlisted in Co. F, 64th Reg. as a 1st Lieutenant. Russell was wounded in the right hip and groin area during the battle of Deep Bottom, Virginia on August 16, 1864. The wound left him partially paralyzed. He practiced law after the war. *Georgia Confederate Pension Applications, 1879–1960*, 11 October 1889, R. A. Russell.

thunderstruck with astonishment but not frightened an atom. I will briefly relate the cause of the disturbance. An order from Head Quarters demanded 82 men from or regiment to act in the capacity of sharpshooters (I Company not being full it did not apply to it) Two or three captains refused to give up the men. They were... [rest of letter missing]

Barnesville, July 30, 1862

My dearest Husband

Your expected letter did not arrive, so you know I have not heard from since you left. I should have been very uneasy but I thought perhaps you did not start your letter in time to reach our office by Saturday mail. I hope this has been the case and nothing serious has happened. I am now at Barnesville and am anxiously expecting a letter on the noon train. I do hope it will come and relieve my anxiety. Father and I came to town this morning purposely to hear from you, he seems anxious too. When you write again be sure to send your letters off on Wednesday or Thursday as the mail to Johnstons stops in Forsyth to be sorted out. Consequently, it lays over just twenty four hours. My dear if you should mail a letter on Friday, Saturday, Sunday Monday, let it be to Barnesville and I will be pretty sure to get them. We have just heard of the capture of Murfreesboro,[36] one of Pa's neighbors was killed in the charge. I suppose they are preparing for another great battle at Richmond. God grant our arms the victory, yes a more brilliant victory than before. My love I went to see Cousin N yesterday. He let me have five shs of nice

---

[36] Under the leadership of General Nathan Bedford Forrest, Confederate forces attacked three Union camps, a Union hospital, and the jail housed in the courthouse. The Macon Telegraph reported that 125 Union soldiers were killed and about 1,250 prisoners were taken: "The depot at Murfreesboro, along with a large lot of new clothing and near a half million dollars' worth of Quartermaster's and Commissary stores were burned. Several railroad bridges near Murfreesboro were also burnt." "The Murfreesboro Affair," Macon (GA) *Telegraph*, 25 July 1862, 77.

lamb's wool that will be enough to make you a full suit. I am going to work on it tomorrow, will you want a vest made, too? I must make you another flannel shirt, perhaps may have enough wool to make one after I make my janes. My love don't you want a box of fruit, I expect to send you a box the first or middle of next week. I wish I could send you some good ripe peaches every day while they last. I visit the orchard often and always think of you and wish you could be with me to eat peaches. My darling I do hope you will be quite well when you receive this letter. I am very very anxious to hear from you it seems like a little age since you left. Tell L.B. if you should be sick he must wait on you the very best until I can get there. My love you remember the "Old Lady" was in quite a stew the morning you left, well I made it convenient to tell her how she had acted in a few days, She owned up, she said she new she had done wrong and asked me to forgive her I did so and we have been very friendly ever since. She says she don't want me to stay anywhere but there, rather seems more cheered up than when we first came out. I expect to stay with him nearly all the while. We have had no rain since you were here, farms in great want of a shower now. You knew that I had forgotten you were here. My love, I left a space to fill after the reception of your letter, but the cars have come and gone. I have sent to the office, but alas! no fond missel came. How can I bear this hard disappointment? I shall leave town for Pa's for a few hours, sad enough will be my homeward march; I can scarcely write I am so sad I hate to write you a sad letter, but you must excuse this time. I have not lost all hope, perhaps a letter may come soon and relieve my aching heart. If you had not left so feeble I would not be so uneasy but I know how you were when you left. I cannot write more, time and sadness of heart forbids the task. If I could hear from you my darling, I think I think I should be content – do write as soon as you get this - if you have not written - and let me know how you are. I mailed a letter to you last Saturday but can't tell whether it has ever reached you. My love I fear you are sick and can't write – do write or get someone else to write for the relief of your fond and anxious wife

MF Ely

P.S. Lizzie is not well, has the scarletina very badly. Eddie and myself are well. Your affectionate M.F. Ely

Camp Way, near Savannah, August 1, 1862

My dearest love,

Your very kind and loving letter was rec'd this morning & I demonstrated my punctuality by replying the same day. I am mortified that my letter did not reach you and extremely sorry you have been so uneasy on my account. This is the third letter I have written since I left you. The first one I directed to Johnstonville – together with a package of papers to your father. My next letter to you was directed to Barnesville. I also mailed another package of papers to your father. I have been thus particular in letting you know how I mailed my letters in order that you may know I haven't failed in my promises or neglected my beloved wife in any way. I am happy to say to you my love that in the midst of much sickness I am in the enjoyment of my usual health. I do not make this announcement boastfully but with a humble grateful heart. I feel sad as often as I think of my little daughter. I eagerly inquired of a Physician the nature of the disease & when he informed me that it was nothing to be alarmed about my fears were very much relieved. I trust when I hear from her again she will be well. My love the sickness in our regiment has not abated. Out of 860 men we have between 500 & 600 men sick or unfit for duty. I shall mention some of the sick you know in our company. Brawner, Hart, Land, Rodgers, Blackmar at home – sick – McLeroy, Whitehead, Branson &c up at Milesville 30 miles above Savannah. Besides we have quite a number of cases in camp and at the hospital about Savannah. W. Brannon and Nathan McLeroy are dangerously sick... [rest of letter missing]

Saturday, August 7, 1862

My Darling Husband,

Your precious letter was received two days ago. I was expecting it several days before its arrival, I have received only two letters from you since you left, am expecting one tomorrow perhaps it come before I send this off, hope so, for I am getting exceedingly anxious to hear from my love again. Honey you don't know half how I prize the privilege of writing and reading letters too and from you, indeed it is all I care for unless it better to send you something to eat or to prepare some article of ____ for your comfort. Yes, there is one other thing; I love to think of you, pray for you, for your safety while away from home and final return from my embrace. My love I received a letter from Jerry a few days since he had been sick two weeks with measles, but was then mending slowly, he is still at Camp Randolph.[37] I have written to Sis Sallie. I am very sorry Mary has taken such a foolish _____, I will try to get her a home and shake her out here if I can. I expect Cous. Nancy has been a little too exacting; but I don't think Mary entirely clear; however I will try what I can do for her about there – I could hire her to Mrs. Pounds, but I am afraid she will be too severe. Mrs. P is without a negro woman. I guess Mary had better stay where she is. I think if Pa would talk to her and Cous Nancy the thing might be compromised and Cous Nancy be induced to become a little more lenient in her discipline. I wish you would write to Pa concerning the above matter and urge him to attend to it immediately. I dislike the trouble of moving Mary so far to stay for so short a time. I expect to make arrangements for housekeeping sometime in Nov. or Dec. My love I have given you my ideas above – now what do you think best? Honey, don't you want some good cider? Pa prepared some yesterday and I would send you a big drink if I could it is so good warm first – getting sharp, and sparkling. Oh, how I wish you had some, it is delightful. I have just taken a drink. Pa is stilling his fruit – has

---

[37] A group of Confederate camps in Gordon County near Calhoun; undated, summer 1862. Smedlund, *Campfires of Georgia Troops, 1861–1865*, 233.

brought home twenty gallons of apple brandy, will have about forty of peach. What is brandy worth in Savannah? Pa speaks of engaging it – about $4.00 per gallon; it is selling for that in Barnesville. I have written to Forsyth for him in order to ascertain the price there. My darling I have succeeded in getting the wool dyed for your clothes, will commence working on it tomorrow, I guess. The children have just kissed me for you, but I can't enclose it. They are so bad, I don't know what to do with them. We have just had a delightful shower, and they are wanting to play under the gutter as usual. I mailed a letter to you last Saturday, and received yours on Sunday. I was expecting it several days before, but - there was no passing from this neighborhood to Barnesville. I guess I shall stay at home until my cloth is prepared for the loom. Did the taylor take your measure for vest and pants. I guess I shall not want the buttons before you come to bring them. I can't get the cloth woven much under a month from this time. I will write then if I want them before. There will be a box at the depot next Tuesday or Monday, I would have sent it off tomorrow but could not get the butter. My love let me know when you want everything. You must write immediately to your Loving wife Mattie Ely

Undated Summer 1862

[Partial letter]

My love you spoke of having cider to drink. If you should have any more you must drink my part & yours too. My love you asked the price of peach brandy in Savannah. I enquired & was told that it would bring 5 to 6 dollars a gal but it could not be shipped here on account of marshall law. Some of the officers told me to say to your father if he would send them 10 galls brandy in a keg nicely boxed up they would pay him 50 Dollars for it you could get your Bro Will to attend to it. My dear I enclosed you some postage stamps in a previous letter but as you do not use them I fear you did not get the letters. However I know you have not received all letters I have written you since my return to camp. My love I have just heard from Pa's. All well – our little crop pretty good. Needham McLeroy[38] is here on a visit. His son Matthew is still very low. Last night we thought he was dying. But he revived and seems a little better today. There is now a faint hope of his recovery. The rest of our sick are convalescing. Lem Brawner is still at home sick. He will return to camp in a week. My love I think I shall be with you again in two or three weeks. It really seems that I have not seen you my precious darling and my sweet little children in six months. Oh! That this horrible war would come to a speedy close that I could again enjoy the sweet companionship of my beloved wife and children. I am not selfish. I desire this also – for the sake of my fellow soldiers to accomplish this I am willing to fight the Yankees a week without resting. In fact I had rather fight the Yankees anytime than to have a spell of fever. Saw the Watson boys yesterday Both well. Kiss the children – Love to all. Write soon and often.

My Love

Your letter came to hand before I could get this off. I was glad you may be sure for I have been a little anxious about that affair below Savannah. I hope, however the ___ is ended, and you will not have to participate; if you should however, you will give them fits. Sorry to hear of so much sickness among the boys. I feel profoundly thankful for your restoration to health, hope it may continue to improve. Lizzie is about well, the salts I gave her had the desired effect. We are all well now. Father has received two bundles of papers, received one last Saturday was very proud of them. I hope the old Yanks will get hurt when they get to Savannah, my darling you must dodge the bullets, if you should get into a battle, I would not have one of those accused balls to hit you for all the gold in the universe. Take care of your precious self my precious one. I

---

[38] Needham McLeroy was a close neighbor of "Pa" Osborn Ely (Marcus's father). They both lived in Mulberry Grove, Harris County. *1860 U.S. Federal Census, Georgia, Harris County*, Mulberry Grove, 77.

am looking forward to a happy reunion in the future that it could take place tomorrow how I would rejoice! I have written the letter in the dark, don't know whether you can read it or not. I have written this in a great hurry, wanting to send it off soon in the morning. I hope I shall not get disappointed this time, Give my sympathies to the sick boys of my acquaintance. I am sorry for them all, hope they will be well soon. I believe I have written all I have in store to write.

Write often to your faithful and Devoted Wife Mattie Ely

Savannah, August 11, 1862

My dearest love,

Your expected letter of the 7th inst. was duly received - was extremely happy to hear from you & not wishing to keep you looking in vain for a letter I take the opportunity of replying. In my last letter I stated that I had just recovered from an attack of bilious fever but was convalescing. I have almost recovered my usual health. In fact I might say that I am well & have a better appetite than I have since I have been in camps. My love I stated in my last letter that our regiment was on eve of moving to White Bluff 9 miles below Savannah. I also stated that Lt. Brewster and I were on the eve of going down to make arrangements for you and Mrs. B to come down to that delightful summer retreat and spend a couple of months with us. Well we went down and rented a pretty good house with four rooms at 10 dollars a month. I expect to borrow a bedstead & have bedding shipped from home & buy a few cheap chairs. Lt. B expected to bring a woman down to do the cooking &c. But just at this time an order came for our regiment to march forthwith to Beaulieu[39] 13 miles from Savannah Ga. on the coast. Accordingly our regiment this morning took up the line of march for

[39] Camp Beaulieu was located on the Vernon River about 12 miles south of Savannah. The camp was situated across from the island of RoseDhu (Rose Dew). Part of the 54th Regiment located there in August 1862. Smedlund, *Campfires of Georgia Troops*, 63.

Beaulieu. Quite a number of us were left behind to take care of the camp &c. The wagons are taking off our camping arrangements as fast as possible. I presume we will all go down tomorrow or next day to join our regiment. My love, we may be able to get a house at Beaulieu but that is in the future. I will wait for my next letter to give you particulars. Beaulieu is a beautiful Savannah resort on Vernon River which is an arm of the sea. There is a battery[40] at that place which our arrangements for you to come down and spend a few weeks with me you should not apprehend any danger as I would not carry you where there was danger… [rest of letter missing]

Camp at Beaulieu, August 17, 1862

My dearest love,

Since reception of your last letter I have written several times, but have not received any reply. I am very uneasy indeed. Last night I sat up until nearly midnight waiting for the courier to come down from Savannah with the mail for the regiment. And when _______ came there was no letter for me. I retired to my cot sad and disappointed. I know that your facilities for mailing letters are bad but I hope they will be better in the future. You perceive from the heading of my letter that we have pitched our camp at Beaulieu. This is a delightful, shady & healthy place on the Vernon River. Said river is about half a mile wide and an arm of the sea. In fact we are in sight of the noble Atlantic. We have a battery just below our camp & in sight of it. On day before yesterday morning the Yankee vessels ran up in less than two miles & turned loose their heavy rifled cannons on our battery. Several of their shots and shells struck quite near the battery. We could see a heavy volume of smoke rise from the vessels, and a few seconds afterwards came the deep booming

---

[40] A Civil War battery consisted of six cannons with over 100 men. A Confederate battery was a bit smaller, numbering only four cannons. Each man in the battery had multiple duties: they had to take care of the horses, guns, and gun carriages. Wright, *The Language of the Civil War,* 23.

thunder followed by the shrieking howling shell, which would explode with a thunderous noise. We all turned out to see the fun. Several of the more active boys climbed to the top of the tall trees to get a good view. Our boys at the battery did not notice the scoundrels and they turned about and left after firing six or 8 shots. We have not seen them since & we do not expect a fight in a long time if ever. My love you must direct your letters as usual as we send a courier to Savannah every day or two. My darling I wish you were here to take salt water baths & eat fish with me. We have a cast net & can get as many fish as we want every day – plenty of mullet and also crab and shrimp. I eat every sort of fish and my appetite is sufficient to ______ me to gnaw the horns off a billy goat. Bro James has come down and joined our company I'll write a _______ ________ paper is very scarce at this place. I forgot to tell you that our company with one other in the regiment (Co. D) will take charge of that battery. Some of the boys are pleased and some are not. I shall stay in my position. The adjutant told me this morning that he would not part from me and he would appoint another man (Billy Brown from Macon) to help me so you can see I do not intend to work the battery but figures. My love my health is very good I wrote to you that I had a pretty tight spell of fever but I am now quite well.

Bob Beal has got back – his sister has gone to Alabama. Dr. Brewster is in Savannah sick. Capt. Russell home on a month's furlough. I shall be at home with you in 8 or 10 days if furloughs do not play out. Write soon and often my love to your affectionate and devoted husband.

MBE

[Written on top of letter]

My love there is a beautiful summer retreat in a mile of our camp called Montgomery. It is on Vernon River. If I get you a boarding place for a month will you come down? I think there is no change in the ________. Let Murphy send his fruit so I can get the sutler to sell them for him and make him a pile of money paying freight damage &c. My love if you sent the box of fruit I did not get it. I sent to the depot every day. Yes I looked over the freight lists in the Savannah papers. Also don't send it my dear if it is not convenient. Tell my boy – no- my big man that I have got a canteen and a little axe for him. Also, a canteen for sister to bring grandpa a cool drink of water from the spring.

Camp William at Beaulieu, August 20, 1862

My Dearest Love,

My anxiety was removed yesterday by the arrival of your letter dated 18th inst. I think it has been about two weeks since I have heard from you and of course I was fearful that you or the children were sick; therefor you can imagine how happy I was yesterday to receive your dear letter and get the assurance that you were in the enjoyment of good health. My dearest you say you answer all my letters hence I know you do not get more than half of them, for I write double as many as I receive, I am satisfied that I have not received more than 3 or 4 letters since my return to camp & I think I have written seven or eight at least. I have written to you once since our regiment has been at this place & directed to Barnesville – you get the letters I direct to Barnesville & I shall direct this to Johnstonville. I am afraid your father will miss his regular papers and I am so far from Savannah that I find it difficult to get a supply. I will however send him a package this week if I can possibly get them, will continue to send them if possible. Our regiment has been very small but it is rapidly increasing. Col. Way[41] has stopped approving furloughs for a while. The reason is -the men go home on furlough and do not return – feign sickness. As soon as the men get in, furloughs will be granted as usual. I hope my darling to be with you by the 10th or the middle of September. My love as you can not leave home in less than three weeks there will be ample time for me to make some arrangements for you and the children to come down. There will be no chance to board

[41] Colonel Charlton Way presided over the 54th GA regiment (see People and Places). Henderson, *Roster of the Confederate Soldiers,* 5:620–21.

at Beaulieu as there is but one house and that is in 50 yds. of the Battery. There is a village on Vernon River about a mile up that is a beautiful place. I shall go up there and ascertain what can be done. My love I have not received that box. I shall try to get it down today however I am almost certain that the fruit has rotted as the box was sent ten days ago. I went to the freight depot several times before we left Savannah but it had not arrived. I am very sorry I was not able to get it at first. We do not get any fruit down at this place. My love there are thousands of oranges at an island about half a mile from our camp. They will soon be ripe & if the Yanks don't keep guard over there I'll send you a box. The mail is about to leave. I must close. I have written in such haste that I have not given you any news – not in fact written anything worth notice. I am well.

Your devoted husband Marcus B. Ely

My love to all Kiss the children have two canteens for Eddy & Lizzie will bring them when I come

August 30, 1862

My Precious Husband,

Your dear letter of the 25th was received day before yesterday. This is the very first opportunity I have had of responding. I was truly glad to hear from my darling once more your letters are like a refreshing shower on a burning desert. I am truly sorry you meet with so many disappointments – my darling I would prevent it all if I could. I think the old freight ought to have a sound drubbing for letting your fruit rot on the way. I cannot imagine why my letters are so long in reaching you. I have been accustomed to sending them off in the early part of the week. My darling, Father has been quite sick for nearly two weeks. I have been here all the while watching him, he is now mending, but slowly. I have been here sitting with him for three nights – past – 'all alone' as no one in the neighborhood knows he is so sick. The Dr. has been tending on him all the week. I think he has some kind of slow fever but hope it is now broken up. We received a letter from Bro. Jerry at the same time with yours, he is still quite low the man who wrote (Mr. Graves)[42] seems to think he is improving slowly. Montgomery's Bat has left camp to join Bragg's division. Jerry was left in camp sick with a few others. I am so uneasy about him, fear he will not have any attention shown him if Graves gets well enough to do duty. I know Bro. is very sick were he not - he would have written himself. Hope to hear from him again soon. I do not know about going into camps at Savannah Pa says he don't think it a fit place for women, however I think I shall try it, - a short time at least if a respectable crowd of ladies will join me. I should like much better more it – not – for being troubled with children. I am afraid Eddy and Lizzie would get drowned in the tide, however we will discuss the subject when you come up. I will try to be prepared to return with you but don't think I can since I have been so much delayed by Pa's sickness. I have little this week but tend on him. I am not afraid of the old Yanks, they will not prevent my coming down. I am glad your health is improving, think you ought to get full after eating so many fish. My love, you must excuse a dull letter, as I don't go a hen's scratch from the door and of course can't pick up any news. I have just received a letter from Sis Sallie, I will include it. The children often speak of you Lizzie counts the days, so does her ma. My darling I am so anxious to hear from you, hope to get a letter this evening. Write soon my precious to your loving and devoted wife Mattie F Ely

Camp Williams, September 9, 1862

My Dearest Love,

I was so sure of getting a furlough a few days ago that I did not write my usual weekly letter to Johnstonville. I was, however, disappointed in getting off, will briefly state the cause of my failure. All the boys in our company who have gone home recently got sick and do

[42] Thomas Graves was a fellow soldier in Jerry Dumas's battalion (see People and Places). *Compiled Service Records of Confederate Soldiers Who Served in Organizations from the State of Georgia,* National Archives, Catalog ID 58695, T.J. Graves.

not return at the expiration of their furlough. They stay as long as they please and those of us in camp are not allowed to go home until those parties return. About two weeks ago I assisted several boys in getting furloughs, told them to come back promptly as I wanted to go. They are still at home, sick or pretending to be. I shall most assuredly be the next man in our company to get a furlough. Think I shall come out in a week, but can not positively say that. I can get off as soon as I have specified. In the meantime my love you must get ready to come back with me. I say this camp is the place for a man's wife provided further more that she has pleasant comfortable quarters at some distance from the regiment camp & again provided further more that she wants to be with her husband. Make your arrangements to come back with me my love. But, if when we talk this thing over, if we decide that it's best for you to stay away then we will abide the decision. I have a large double tent fixed up near the adjutant's tent. Quite a large number of officers have their wives with them & some, in fact, nearly all of them are in their tents. There are Capts. Brantley, Clarke, Burkes wives here, also Col. Ways and Adjt. Brantley.[43] Several privates are making arrangements to get their wives here. This is perhaps one of the healthiest spots on the globe. If you can come down I shall hire a negro boy to mind the children. In concluding this matter will say that I do not intend to persuade you but have you decide. My darling, I have received your letter announcing the death of your dear brother.[44] I cannot describe to you how sadly it made me feel or how deeply & truly I sympathize with you. My dear and precious wife, he was all that was generous, pure and noble. All that was lovely and attractive was centered in him. But, he is gone and truly may we say that a good man has fallen. It then behooves us all to cherish his dear memory and emulate his rare virtues. Bro. James has been quite feeble for some

---

[43] Officers of the 54th Regiment included Colonel Charlton Way; Thomas M. Brantley, Adjutant; Major William Mann; Captain Thomas A. Burke, Quartermaster; and Captain John G. Clarke, Commissary. Henderson, *Roster of the Confederate Soldiers,* 5:620–21.

[44] "Your dear brother" referred to Jerry Dumas.

time but not confined to his tent. The surgeon would not excuse him from duty. I shall give said rascal (the surgeon) a little plain simple talk – even if I am put on bread and water for a month and hereafter when Bro. J is on guard & complaining of being sick, I shall take his place. My dear it is a source of great happiness that you and the children still enjoy good health. Glad Father Dumas is improving. My health is good except for a boil on my heel – can hardly walk – although it is not so very painful. I can tell you many things should you come out. I have been on a scout over on Burnside Island, found oranges growing in [rest of letter unreadable]

Your affectionate husband, MBE

Camp Williams, October 3, 1862

My Dearest Love,

I was aroused this morning by reveille and the first thing I thought of was the reception of your very welcome letter of the evening before. I hasten to reply fearing that I shall not be able to get the letters in the morning mail to Savannah. I shall be brief this morning for several reasons among the most prominent - want of time & something interesting to write I expect to write again in a very short time, perhaps in two days. Say to Mr. Matthew Gibbs[45] I have ascertained where Messrs Martin & Stou are located and will send their letter to them today. A gentleman told me he did not think they had made much salt yet as they have not fully completed their preparations. Say to Bro. Will I have been so busy since I returned that I have not visited any of the salt works except one. I went to Mess Johnston Cookes & Co. yesterday. They would not sell at any price- been selling sometime ago at 15.00 per bushel. Say to Bro. Will I shall visit all the salt works[46] in my reach and

[45] Matthew Gibbs was a neighbor of Moses Dumas (Mattie's father). 1860. *US Federal Census, Georgia, Monroe County*, 9.

[46] Early in the war, there was concern about salt shortages in the south. Salt was an essential commodity for food preservation, leather tanning, and

then write to him before buying in a very few days Will also send to Savannah to see about the ~~twine~~ ~~tw~~ flax. Tell him I have not been able to do anything with my seine however a seine is not worth much here. A small party of soldiers went out in a boat yesterday morning and caught 449 fish in a few hours with a hook & line, I caught a fine mess not so many fish but they were large – am going again this morning. My love I do not like to write you a dry letter but such is the case. I will try to be more entertaining in the next I believe want to see you worse than ever also the children I will write a long letter by Tuesday mail also to Bro Will The Yankees were shelling Fort Jackson below Savannah yesterday but have not heard of the scoundrels accomplishing anything.

Goodbye my love Write soon & often to your Affectionate Husband MBEly

Camp Williams, Beaulieu, October 11th 1862

My Dearest Love,

My anxiety was relieved this morning by the appearance of your dearly esteemed letter. I was very uneasy indeed fearing you were sick as I had not received a letter in some time in fact I had received but one since before I returned to camp. I much rejoiced to hear from you & the children & final to hear that you and they enjoy good health. My love there is some mystery about our letters. I am satisfied that I do not get all your letters nor do you get all of mine. However, I will not discuss that question now. My love I have taken a rather long journey today visiting the salt works. There now I have broken my pencil … Well to go back to the salt works. I found none that sold for less than $20.00 per bushel. It may be worth thirty or forty dollars by next week. At Thunderbolt I

---

household use. The Union blockade caused a spike in salt prices. At the beginning of the war, a 150-pound sack of salt cost 50 cents; by 1863 the price of salt was fifty times as much in Savannah. Union attacks on salt works on the coast and in Florida further reduced the supply of salt. The deliberate destruction of salt works in the South limited the amount of food that could be preserved, reducing the food supply for troops and civilians. Varhola, *Life in Civil War America*, 165.

understand one company is selling at $8.00 per bushel. But have heard several gentlemen say it is not worth giving away as it is yellow and dirty and would not salt pork. I am very much perplexed about this matter. I do not care for the trouble, but I am afraid I cannot give satisfaction. I think the best plan is to send the money back by express and let the parties buy Liverpool salt even if it is $40.00 a bushel, as I have serious doubts about the coast salt curing meat. Please show this to Bro. Will & the rest also to Mr. Gibbs. My dear I am delighted to hear the time of your visit is so near. I want you to come my love just as soon as possible, don't delay a single day and if Cousin Fannie will come bring her along & she can enjoy herself finely here_ Tell her we do nothing but frolic around. No Yankees to fright nothing to do but eat beef & enjoy ourselves generally. My love in your next state when you will leave so that I can meet you in Savannah. Stay in Macon for the night train and I will meet you in Savannah at the Pulaski House[47] next day. Also let me know if you want any money. If so & you have not time to write to get it, let me know or get what you need from Bro Will Dumas & will express it to him immediately. I shall have your quarters all ready. Write soon to your most affectionate husband MBE

I will write again in a few days perhaps in two days

Camp near Beaulieu, December 2, 1862

My dearest Love,

Again as we are separated by many long weary miles and again I grasp my pen to have a little chat through the measure of epistlatory correspondence and again this is by the way my greatest consolation in our absence. I trust you reached home safe and sound without fatigue or

---

[47] Pulaski House was an elegant hotel in Savannah. The hotel, established in 1835, was located at Bull and St. Julian's Street at Johnston Square. "Pulaski House," Georgia Archives, Georgia's Virtual Vault, last modified 2015, http://cdm.georgiaarchives.org:2011/cdm/singlei tem/collection/vg2/id/3702/rec/2.

accident and I further more hope that the exposure you have been subjected to in camp will not affect your health. My love when you and I separated Sunday night at the Depot I went to the 32nd Ga Regiment & spent the night. Next morning I went uptown and very soon ascertained that the chances for getting conveyance to Beaulieu were rather gloomy. I was therefore compelled to walk back which I accomplished in a reasonable time with no other inconvenience save sore feet. On Monday I went to the river and fished with pole &line – caught about 40 or fifty nice fish I wanted you to have them but could not send them. My love I felt very sad when I pass our old tent I passed yesterday and looked for the children's tracks in the ashes. I did not see them & felt relieved for if I had seen their tracks I would have felt sadder than ever. Today I am 31 years old you ought to make me a present. By the way I lost my gloves on the omnibus. If you can replace them as a birthday present you will confer a lasting benefit &c Write soon my love and write often to your affectionate Husband My love to all Marcus B Ely

Camp near Beaulieu, December 6, 1862

My Dearest Love,

Your letter came in due Season and I was not disappointed – was quite happy to learn that you had reached home Safe, in good health &c You stated that you were uneasy about certain Yankee ships &c You need entertain no fears. Those vessels have all left and are now off the coast of North Carolina. It is thought they design cooperating in the attack on Richmond. Hence they will probably defer making an attack on Charleston or Savannah until after Christmas and in the event they should fail to reduce Richmond they may postpone it indefinitely. At all events it is generally believed that they are now preparing to make one last deathly struggle (which they will fail) to give up the contest. I wish there was a little spark of hope for peace. This separation from home and all its Joys is a very unpleasant business. But as old Gabriel says "There is no other" all eternity but to wait and fight and endure until something turns up that will bring about the desired end. My love - as far as your trade is concerned I hardly know what to think about it. I shall not at present condemn the measure but will let you know soon what is best to be done. If I could raise the money I would not say a word but I am afraid I cannot get it. I will write to Pa to know if he has any on hand. It would probably be best to sell her if you can get her worth but you may wait until you hear from me again. No news in the regiment. You must recruit for our company. We have nearly a hundred men in our company and if there are any men in Monroe or Pike who wish to join a good company on the coast they had better come soon before the enrolling officer gets them. Kiss the children. I am so cold I must close. Will try to come at Christmas. Have sent on Jud's transfer and will have him with us soon. Love to all Write soon my dear I am always on the lookout for your dear billet doux's.

Yours devotedly, MB Ely

P.S. You and the children must be vaccinated without delay as you are running much risk my dear MBEly

Camp near Beaulieu, December 16, 1862

My dearest wife,

Your letter has just made its appearance and after reading the precious lines from my absent loved one I hasten to reply. My dear I wrote to you last night – stating the utter impossibility of getting a leave of absence of any kind. I am very sorry and mortified indeed, that I cannot meet you in Macon at the specified time. However there is no remedy, & I am compelled to make the most of a bad matter. My darling I shall be very brief this time, you received all the news &c in my last letter. You must go to Perry without me. You may do well to get advice from your Bro Will as to the proper manner in which you should act. In the first place the note he (Bro J) holds against the estate must be produced, or it will and void after the settlement on the 22nd Dec. I suppose now my dear it will not be necessary for me to send any money to you. If however, it is necessary you must make some arrangements until I get the money I send home often. Of course our relatives will make some allowance for a poor soldier in the war who cannot even get a furlough to attend to a little business. It may be Christmas before the money is sent to me. You will get it however just as soon as I can express it to you after its reception. My love all the troops about Savannah but our regiment and a few companies have received marching orders & gone nobody knows where – perhaps to Virginia – where the great battle is now being fought & where Southern independence will be achieved – May God speed the Right – May he lend us his right arm in in defense of our beloved South that our army may hurl them into everlasting perdition to avenge the death of our beloved General T.R. Cobb.[48] I enclose you a note from Mrs. Way. No new cases of small pox. Write to your affectionate husband MB Ely

Barnesville, December 24, 1862

My Darling Husband,

I have just returned from a trip to Perry and was disappointed of not meeting you. I expected to find a letter of late date from you on my return but disappointment, disappointment. I have drank thy cup to the bitter dregs!! My love I wrote to you while in Perry (last Thursday I believe) stating the time I expected to leave for Forsyth. My love I heard last Sunday morning while in Macon, Way's Reg had been ordered to Carolina since I have heard nothing from Savannah all is as silent (and almost as gloomy with me) as the grave itself. I see from your last letters (two of which awaited me on arrival dated the sixteenth. The other on the fifteenth) no more furloughs are to be granted and my happy anticipations are doomed to sad, sad disappointment. How I hoped you would be here to eat "Christmas dinner" with me, but now I shall eat no Christmas dinner! My soul shall be sad, sad all the while I will not, I cannot be gay, for too deep a gloom is already hovering like a dark pall around my heart – My precious you asked me to enjoy myself and think of you, I can and will comply with the latter request but not the former is

[48] General Thomas R. R. Cobb, an Athens citizen and Confederate general, died in the battle of Fredericksburg, Virginia on December 13, 1862. "Death of General T.R.R. Cobb," *Daily Constitutionalist* (Augusta GA), 14 December 1862, 3.

all forgiven to me at this time, think you I could be merry when you are away. My love tomorrow is my birthday and a sad one it will be the saddest birthday I have ever spent. I know I feel more like my funeral was going to be preached. Precious you must pardon the sad tone of this letter that is if you ever receive it, which I doubt very much as I don't know where to direct it. You may now be among the cold leaves of "Old Virginia" awful thought – however I will direct to Savannah thinking maybe it will be forwarded to you. Yes darling, there are your socks and gloves, I expected you could get them when you came to see me – but now your hands and feet are now probably suffering with cold. I would express your things to you if I only knew where you are. Do write and let me know where you are. Nothing can be done with Brother Jerry's business as no one has yet administered on the estate. I guess all will remain as it is until you come home. I will write down to the ordinary requesting him to appoint someone administrator now that you can't come home. Brother's <u>copartenership</u> farming interest is looming more than anything else. I haven't the slightest confidence in the surviving partner though. I will write to some friends to see after the farming interest. I brought Brother's trunks away with me; he left a nice lot of clothing, shoes, boots &c, and also several pieces of furniture as the latter I did not move, but left in the care of his land lady. My darling there will be several hundred dollars worth coming to us if affairs are properly managed. Love, I will leave for Harris just as soon as I can get money to make the trip. You wrote that you would express me some in a few days if however you cannot ________ enough to pay off my indebtedness, I can sell the old woman I bought from the Estate, but I much prefer we could keep her as she would suit for a cook and for a house woman finally. I wish you could be here to move me out to Harris, if I keep the woman had I not better write Pa word to send a wagon out after the negroes and plunder? Write in your next letter what I had best do for I can't think what will be best. I know that your decision will be mine. However, I have resolved to return to my little farm and do the very best I can until you, which I hope will be very soon. Maybe by planting time. God grant it may is my daily prayer. My love, give my love to Mrs. Way and tell her I have not yet succeeded in getting thread fine enough for the manufacture of her dry goods. I will make every effort to get up her dress but I am afraid I will not succeed after all. however I will not leave a stone unturned and if I do not succeed I will let her know. Now my darling, I have written a long letter but I fear you will never receive it, however if you should be so fortunate as to get said letter, be sure to write immediately to your faithful and loving Wife, M.F. Ely

P.S. We are all well don't be uneasy about us.

Camp near Beaulieu, December 26, 1862

My Darling Wife,

I have just finished the perusal of your dear letter which was read with unspeakable satisfaction. I am very much mortified my dear that you should have spent any unhappy moments under the misapprehension that our Regiment had gone to Virginia. I am glad to inform you that we are still at old Beaulieu and will probably remain here all winter- and for aught I know to the contrary, till the end of the war. Like yourself my darling I can not but hope that this unnatural and unholy war is fast approaching its end. The hated foe have already acknowledged that all is "black despair" If that be the case we can readily surmise that the word "enough" is not far from their sin polluted life. In their desperation and madness they have called for a hundred negro regiments which demonstrates conclusively that they have lost confidence in their white troops and they now wish to send negroes down south to fight us. Such an idea! A people so lost to all sense and reason must be infatuated by the devil and led captive at his will. For them there is no redemption in this world My love you want to know what you had better do in regard to going home &c I think it would be advisable for you to remain where you are for a few days. I think there will be a chance for me to get a furlough in a short time. They are granting some furloughs already. I heard Lt. Brewster left on a furlough this evening. My business is as urgent as his. I have as good a right to go home on business as he has. I shall make an application in a week or ten days from this time and I trust it will be granted. I shall, also, if I get a furlough make arrangements to pay for that woman. As I told you in a previous letter I have a portion of the money and will get the balance before I come. If however after making the effort to get off - I should fail-I can then express the money to you. My love I believe the smallpox situation is gradually dying out. The case we had near us is dead. He recovered from the smallpox and died of pneumonia. No other cases as yet – and I trust that one will be the last. I was uneasy about you when you were at Perry knowing that you were in the vicinity of the small pox. You must be on your guard and subject yourself to no danger. My love, as I am writing a Christmas letter, I should be most happy to make it interesting but I fear when I finish it that the only remarkable feature about it will be its length. We have had some Christmas even in camp- Last night Capt Russell gave his company an eggnog – It cost nearly fifty dollars and did not average a glass to each of his men. Quite a number of the officers and men were on a regular "bust" The sutler's tent was thrown down and other mischief done in so much that a double guard was stationed around the camp. The guard or at least a portion of them were slightly tight and kept up such a hubbub calling the corporal &c, that I could not sleep much. Besides I was quite sick last night but feel better. Rec'd a letter from Judson this evening. Blackmon has not yet reported and the poor fellow is very low in spirits. He is at Wilmington, says the weather is bitterly cold and he has no overcoat or gloves. He sent his overcoat home last Spring. I am very sorry for him but I trust he will be with us soon. His regiment is comfortably quartered in houses – Judson thinks they will go to Virginia, but I think they will remain where they are as Wilmington is a threatened point - Honey, I do sincerely trust that there will be no difficulty in getting a furlough for I've never wanted to see you and the children worse in my life. I can probably inform you in my next as to the certainty of my succeeding. About thirty of our men ran away this Christmas. I am afraid they will fare badly when they come back. "Bob Mitchell the ________ together with 14 others have been published as deserters & will probably be shot when they are caught. Lt. Hightower is still absent. Colonel Way has reported him to General Beauregard and he will be dropped in disgrace from the Confederate Army.[49] I shall get the place he vacates but I am no means anxious for it & were it not that there is a good chance for promotion I should remain as I am. Bro. James is in good health. He is commissionary for the Company which relieves him from Guard duty – which you know is the most disagreeable duty a soldier has to perform. My love I complained a little about the "infrequency" of your letters write often my dear – every other day is not too often Kiss the children my dear and write me a long letter and oblige

Your devoted husband MBE

Barnesville, December 27, 1862

Dearest Husband,

Your precious letter dated 24th inst came ___ to hand and I can assure you it met with the warmest imaginable reception. I was vain enough to expect one or two of late date would be waiting my return home so you may form some idea of my disappointment when I found none of later date that 16th inst. My love I wrote you on the 24th inst and a sad letter I know you think it is in fact to tell the truth I was almost crazy. I had just learned that Way's Reg. had been ordered to Carolina, at what point I could not learn. Consequently I feared all clue as to your whereabouts for the ______________. You can't wonder then at the sad tenor of my letter. I hope however you will forgive as I do not often write in so sad a strain. My love I hope your Christmas has passed off pleasantly if you were deprived of coming home we may yet be spared to spend many Christmases together and then we can look back to the one we spent separate, not with pleasure but of one looking from the sunshine of noonday to the darkness of midnight. My dear you asked me to give you my plans for the coming year; have none definitely fixed though my notions for the present is to return to my little farm. We are

[49] William J. Hightower was elected Jr. 2nd Lieutenant July 5, 1862. Ill health forced him to resign on January 7, 1863. Henderson, *Roster of the Confederate Soldiers,* 5:704.

not able to pay board and I feel unwilling to stay on any of our friends. I thought once of returning to camp where I could enjoy your society and I would certainly do so if not for the children. Camps I know is not a fit place for children. My Love I hope you will get off to see me on my way homeward. I expect to leave in about two weeks perhaps sooner. I will write your Father to meet me in Columbus, however I can stay a few days longer if you would think there be any chance for you to come up. My dear father's estate has not yet been wound up, I have not yet made arrangement to take the negro woman I purchased of the estate. I don't think there will be enough coming to me to pay off the note – and for the woman I guess I will be compelled to part with the woman in order to meet the note held by the estate. I expect to see Brother James soon and we will then arrange things between us. My dear you said it was strange for me to expect you in Perry, you will not think so when I tell you I did not receive your last two letters, one dated the 15th the other 16th until I arrived from Perry. Brother Will received a letter from you dated the 20th stating you had expressed him a barrel of oysters. The barrel arrived on the 24th inst but it was not near full. The lid had been broken out and I suppose the public helped themselves. Brother was none the less delighted with his _____ and says he is willing to pay you for them. The Express was four dollars. My love you wrote that you had made arrangements for the payment for a part of my indebtedness. I wish you would send me some money as I cannot pay all my debts and then get home on what I have. You know that I am unwilling to ask one of my brothers to loan me money. I wish your father would send out after me and the children, but I know he will not like to do that. My dear I think that I will have to stay home if I ever get there for one cannot turn without spending money these days. I am no "spend thrift" but somehow I have made away with a pile of money this year without ever receiving any very lasting benefit. Well, my precious I guess you are sorely tired of this _____ so I will change schedule. I received Mrs. Way's note enclosed in yours. Tell her my efforts to procure thread for the manufacture of her goods have hitherto been fruitless, however I will try again when I get home, perhaps I may to be able to secure thread in Columbus if I should be so fortunate. I will make up the goods as soon as I can. My love I have some socks, a pair gloves and a blanket I desire sending you if you wish them. Say, I must send them by Express or shall I wait until you come up. My love I forgot to tell you, I lost my trunk when returning from Perry, have not heard from it sinse it was nearly full of valuables, among the rest – some of Brother James' books and his type. I have written to the proprietor of the Brown House requesting him to look out for it and get it – if possible. I do not expect I will ever hear from it again. I gave the porter my trunk at my room and told him to get my checks. (I had three of brother's trunks.) The porter gave me four checks, but checked a trunk that does not belong to me. My Dear you told me to take _____ by the length of your letter and I think I have this time. I have written until I am "out of soap." Myself and the children are well. They (the chicks) often speak of their Pa. We are all extremely anxious to see you hope we have the pleasure of beholding you face to face in _____ time then one week. Do come if you can possibly get off. Tell Old Mercer you are willing to risk the smallpox. We don't care for it about here. My dear I must close as it will soon be time to mail this letter. Goodbye write soon and often to your devoted Wife Mattie F Ely

Camp near Beaulieu, December 30, 1862

My Dearest Wife

I have given you a few long winded epistles recently and they have had the desired effect – for the dear interesting letter which I rec'd this evening together with one rec'd and answered a few days ago were just such as I always love to get. I was on alert when the mail arrived & when I recognized in the bundle of letters your well known penmanship as is my usual custom I drew a long breath of satisfaction. My last letter (four pages on fools cap[50]) will keep you busy for some time – but I do not

---

[50] Foolscap was a popular size (8 ½ in. x 13 ½ in.) stationery in the nineteenth century. David B. Guralnik, *Webster's New World Dictionary of the American Language* (New York: NY, One World Publishing Co, 1970), 543.

promise that you will be edified or even entertained. It seems that I acted on the principle –"not how well – but how much." My love I shall settle the matter by making the following proposition – that you will respond promptly to every letter you get from me and I will do the same. Dear I think I shall be able to get a furlough in 8 or 10 days. So if nothing unusual happens you may look for me by the 10th of Jan. In the meantime you can remain where you are and make your other arrangements afterward. I hardly know at present what suggestions to make. I am fearful that you will not be satisfied at home by yourself and if you will not consent to go and make Pa's your home I would rather pay your board where you would be satisfied. We will talk of this hereafter. I would come up now or rather I would make an effort to do so but Lt. Hightower will be "dropped or cushiend" in a few days and I understand there will be an election immediately to fill the vacancy. I shall get the place and do not wish to be absent. The election may be postponed if so I'll come up as soon as practical. Adjt. Brantley's wife is with him. Billy Brown's wife is coming again soon. She sent love to you in her letter to Billy. I have not seen Mrs. Way to deliver your messages. The Colonel is in Savannah sick and Mrs. W has not been with us so much this month. Mrs. Mann sends her regards – also her "Spouse" – the Major.[51] Some of the officers frequently ask me when I will bring my "soldier boy" back? I am very anxious to see my soldier boy and soldier girl as well as their mother. Yes honey I do want to see you worse than I ever did in my life. My dear I am very sorry you lost your trunk – think you had better advertise for it, Sorry Bro Will's oysters were disturbed. The barrel was piled full when it left. Will send another barrel if they are worth paying freight on. Tell Brother Will I thought strange of him for offering pay – hope he will not say anything more about paying me. Write soon my love. I am as ever Your affectionate & Devoted MBE

---

[51] William H. Mann was elected Major of the 54th Georgia Infantry on May 16, 1862. He was killed in the Battle of Atlanta on July 22, 1864 (see People and Places).

Camp near Beaulieu, December 31, 8 o'ck PM/62

My Darling Wife

I am the happy recipient of your kind favor which came to hand this evening I assume my love the old year will have a pleasant exit on account of its reception which as usual brought joy and gladness to my heart. I thank you my dear for being so punctual. I shall always reciprocate in order to show my appreciation of your kindness; so that when you look for a letter from me you shall not look in vain. I trust our mail facilities may be as good in the future as they have been heretofore for if I hear from my dear loved ones at home, I could not abide the horror of separation. My love, the old year with so much of sorrow, mourning and lamentation -with so little of joy & gladness – domestic happiness is on the eve of dissolution. A few hours hence, and it will be numbered among the things that were & a new year will be ushered in - whether fraught with __________ or ___________ none but God can tell. My love when we look back upon the year just past we can truly say we have never in our lives witnessed such mighty events or stirring times as those – which will crowd the pages of history in the future. A young and struggling nation cut off from the rest of the world - deprived of many of the luxuries and even some of the necessities of life – contending with a huge giant whose mighty grasp has threatened its life's blood is indeed a theme worthy of contemplation. When Greek meets Greek then comes the tug of war – has been amply demonstrated in this contest – The abolition hordes who have poured down on our beloved soil - have been met with strong arms and strong hearts – and those who came to plunder, burn and destroy have been scattered "like the chaff that the wind driveth" Those same scoundrels – who thought the control of the South an easy victory – have found to their utter dismay "____________ worthy of their steel" – Yes, Superior for they have demonstrated their superiority on many a bloody field from Maryland to the Gulf of Mexico. Love, I hope the new year that tomorrow's dawn will usher in will not witness the many bloody fields of carnage that characterized the old – but may the olive branch be tendered and accepted- that a weary worn nation may lay down its arm and rest in peaceful _____________. Peace—peace oh for peace is the anxious cry of the poor mother & children who think tenderly and sadly of husband and father on the terrible field. Peace—peace is the prayerful desire of the grief stricken parents who have given of their sons to go & battle for their country's cause. Oh! That we could have peace is the oft expected expression of the sentinel on his lonely rounds, and his desire finds an echo in ten thousand hearts. May God grant them their desire and usher in the harbinger of better days.

1863

"I Shall Try to Get a Furlough"

January 1, 1863

Happy New Year My Love

May many joys be in store for you and the little ones and finally – may your old man soon get home to sit with his little family around his own fireside. A freeman in a free and united Southern Confederacy - never to be separated again. If these are not my true sentiments then I am an idiot that's all. My love and regards to Bro. Will and family. Wish I could spend New Years day with all of you. Know I would be as happy as the lark when he tunes his pipe and rises to meet the sun, Goodbye my love and remember

I am yours forever, MBE

[5th page]

My darling as I shall not have the privilege of writing you another letter this year I cannot get my consent to stop just yet – not withstanding I have nothing to communicate worthy of arresting your attention. Happy to inform you that my health which has been feeble for some time is rapidly improving. Have had a few light chills recently and am looking just now a "little the worse for wear" but am rapidly improving in appearance. Brother Judson has at last made his appearance among us. I am certainly glad he has come for the minds of all them at home will be relieved. They have been very anxious for a long time that this transfer should be effective.

Love I hardly know whether I can let you go home or not & this separates us by additional distance. Col. Way asked me this evening when you are coming back and since then I have been asking myself this question when are you coming back By the way you must ask yourself the question and try to answer it satisfactorily to your humble servant. My dear I shall try to get off in a week to see you. I hope that I shall succeed but then I may be disappointed. I think I am a favorite with Col Way & for that reason conclude that he will lend me his influence in getting off particularly as I have pressing business to attend to. When the election comes off in our company, I must be on hand. Hightower will in all probability be dropped around the fifth of January. Col Way will order an election at once to fill the vacancy. If he offers the election I can come home at any time. However I must be governed by circumstances. I shall try in the meantime to determine that I shall make an effort to get a furlough – cautioning you at the same time I may fail. I would send you some money in this letter but for fear of an accident I will wait and if I fail to get off I can express to you.

Barnesville, January 7, 1863

My Dearest Love

Your precious letter came to hand yester eve was perused with delight__________________ just about to travel to Forsyth am in a great hurry consequently you must not expect much of a letter this time. It is so cold that I can scarcely hold my pen, much less guide it steadily. The ground is frozen and sounds like a brick pavement under the tramp of the foot. My dear when you write again direct to Forsyth and when you come up, stop there. I hope your next letter will bring the glad tidings of your return, may you have the utmost success in getting a furlough. Nothing would delight me more than to have you come in fact I can't get along well without you just at this juncture. I have no news to write, however it has been rumored that Bragg was defeated at last if it is true I guess we will hear other particulars today. I feel exceedingly anxious, hope we have not met with so sad a catastrophe. My dear I do wish I had something worth writing, I know you will throw down this letter in disgust. I have nothing to write worth reading - my Love I shall expect you next Saturday noon that is if I'm not informed to the contrary hope I shall not be again disappointed. I know that you will get off if you can. I think that you are anxious to come, yes I know you are. My Love don't trouble about those oysters. We are all facing ______ hog killing

__________________________. I could send you some ribs and backbones but it is so uncertain about you getting them, that I almost despair about ever sending you anything by Express. I could have you some Sunday &c but then they would have to spoil before you could get them and then the Express money would be thrown away as usual. My love don't bring the children any toys. They have more now than they can take care of. Eddie has had his wagon and Lizzie has broken some of her tea things. We are wanting shoes more than anything else but I know you can't get them at Savannah, I will try to have some made in the shop in Forsyth, they make a very nice calf shoe down there for $10 dollars. My calf shoes were stolen out of the trunk with the other goods. The robbery has not yet been traced up, I will try to find some clue to the perpetrators today. Give my love to our brothers, to Mrs. Way and others. All send love. I must close, so Goodbye my precious Excuse this hasty letter of your devoted wife, MFEly

Beaulieu, GA, January 8, 1863

My Darling,

I shall write you a very brief note tonight in reply to yours of ____ _____ which I had the exquisite pleasure of receiving this evening. It is extremely mortifying to forgo the pleasure of seeing you at the time you specified, but love this must be my representative. I briefly stated in my last letter the reasons why I could not come to see you the first of this month, but now fear you failed to get the letter, so I will state them again. Lt. J.W. Hightower has resigned unconditionally and gone home. There will be an election to fill the vacancy in a few days and as I am expecting the position I think it best for me to remain in camp If you will come down and spend a few weeks with me I will give you comfortable quarters and promise to go back with you when you go – will also express you as much money as you need Let me know what you will do my love and also how much money you will need. Mrs. Brown will be down next week Mrs B is very anxious for you to come down Mrs. Way says you must come for she is anxious to see you. Col. Way asked me when you are coming so it seems there is no other chance Dear I am sick tonight and must be brief – I believe this is the shortest letter I have written you since I have been in service -will do better in the future no news Mrs Mann sends love Write your news about this matter my love and believe me

Yours devotedly MBE[1]

Camp near Beaulieu, January 10, 1863

My Darling Wife,

How happy I was tonight to receive your dear dear letter! Your pleasure letter was an agreeable surprise as I was not expecting one before another mail. On day before yesterday I wrote you a short note – hope you will not blame me for its brevity – was somewhat indisposed when it was written. But now am quite well Darling I am so anxious to see you, It really seems an age since you went home I think however my love I can make the trip at the time specified in a previous letter. I do not remember when you left (the day of the month) but it seems were never separated so long before. May the time speedily come when we will be separated no more but I think that time far in the future. My love an order came yesterday from Gen Beauregard[2] Cashining Lt. J W Hightower. An election was ordered today and I was elected to fill the vacancy so that I am now Brevet 2nd Lt. of Co. H. B.B. McCraw[3] was my opponent. He received 14 votes and I rec'd 46 - and at least eight or ten of my friends were absent or I should have beaten him by a still greater majority. Col. Way and Maj Mann were very much interested on my behalf. The Major said he would spend $50.00 to elect me if necessary Capt Russell "spread" himself and was badly frightened -

[1] This letter is in bad shape; it was torn and half is missing.

[2] Gen. Pierre Thomas Beauregard was the 1st Commanding General of the Confederate Forces. He led the attack on Ft. Sumter, South Carolina on April 12, 1861 (see People and Places). Mark M. Boatner, *The Civil War Dictionary* (New York NY: Vintage Books, 1991) 54.

[3] B.B. McCraw was reported absent without leave from February 26, 1863. No further records found. Henderson, *Roster of the Confederate Soldiers*, 5:705.

fearing I would be defeated but I knew how it would result from the beginning. I should not have cared much about the position, had there not been a chance for promotion.

Lt Brewster will get out of service…

Camp near Beaulieu, February 24, 1863

My Dearest,

On yesterday when the mail for the regiment arrived and I was not disappointed. For sometime precious as you are aware, I felt but little interest in the mail, but my interest has suddenly revived. My love I was truly glad to learn that you arrived in Forsyth safely & in the enjoyment of health. Separation is an awful thing but I can bear it so much better when I know that my family are well & doing well. Dear I have not a word of interest to write & I dislike to bore you with a dull & senseless letter. The Yankee Vessels (10) are still lieing off Beaulieu Battery. They are landing on a island about six miles from the Battery. Do not know what they mean and furthermore I do not care. They do not give me any trouble or uneasiness. There are a great many troops in and around Savannah ready and willing to give them just deserts– wherever they show their rotten carcasses. Love this is the dullest place to me I ever saw. In fact I could not feel more lonely were I in the midst of the great desert in Africa. There is an aching void that none but you can fill and I do hope that circumstances will soon warrant me in "ordering" you back to camp. Mr. Brown returned from Macon this morning. He is very much dejected. I sympathize with him. We are still ditching and your humble servant is tired of looking at spades and shovels. I am Officer of the Guard tomorrow. It seems they never forget me - but when my times comes (and it comes very often) they do not slight me. Send me some butter & eggs and I shall be very glad I will send you some money next week if nothing happens. Will write again soon

Love to all Your Devoted Husband MBE

Kiss the children

Beaulieu, February 28, 1863

My Dearest Love,

Another day has past I am sorry to say to inform you that the fine Confederate Steamer (Nashville)[4] that lay in the Ogeechee near Fort McAllister was destroyed this morning to prevent her from being captured by the enemy. The particulars are these: last night she dropped down the river for the purpose of trying to run out sometime during the night. This morning the iron clad and three other vessels steamed up the river and attacked her furiously. She (the Nashville) being aground could not escape it being low tide – the crew was therefore under the necessity of setting her on fire and escaping in their boats. When she blew up the report jarred the earth for many miles around. At the same time the infernal Yankees raised a tremendous shout and dropped down the river to their same old stand. My darling you have not the remotest idea of how I wish to see you and the children. Oh! I am so disgusted with this war. I would rather I could fight out my part of it and go home. But, I try to exercise patience which is at all times a _______ and especially so in this instance. It is now about 9 o'clock and raining very hard. I am not very well shall take medicine tomorrow. Ask Eddy & daughter if they want to come see Pa. My pen is a very poor one. Good by dear precious sweet darling - will write again in two days___

Your most affectionate, MBE

---

[4] The CSS Nashville was originally a passenger steamer built in 1853. She was seized by the Confederacy at Charleston, South Carolina in 1861 and converted to a lightly armed cruiser. Between 1861 and 1862, the Nashville attacked and burned several USN ships. In late 1862 she became a blockade runner, renamed the Rattlesnake. On February 28, 1863 the Rattlesnake tried to outrun the USS Montauk, but ran aground in the Ogeechee River where she was burned. According to the *Macon Telegraph*, the ship was loaded with 700 bales of upland cotton, seventy-seven barrels of rosin, and forty boxes of tobacco. "Nashville Destroyed by the Enemy," *Macon* (GA) *Telegraph*, 3 March 1863, 3.

Beaulieu, March 1, 1863

My Darling Wife,

I wrote you on yesterday stating that I would not write again until the expiration of two days. But my mind changed upon the reception of your dear precious letter which came to hand this evening. I can truly say that your dear letters are the only rays of sunshine that lighten up my dark pathway. I look forward to the time of their arrival with the most profound and even deeply thankful to be assured of the uninterrupted health of yourself and children. Darling there are 18 gunboats and ironclads off Beaulieu Battery. The majority of them came in and dropped anchor this evening. They are now (9 o'clock pm) throwing up their signal lights. Col Way thinks there will be an attack either at Beaulieu Battery or Genesis Point tomorrow & according the old 54th are making all necessary preparations tonight – filling canteens & packing knapsacks &c. In case of an attack on Beaulieu Battery – Lt. Brewster will take 34 men to assist in moving the guns – I & Lt. Beall will take charge of the remainder of the men to form with the regiment in case of a land attack. They may defer an attack tomorrow, but I am dispose to think that they contemplate making a demonstration at some point very soon. You must not be uneasy my dear. I know you want me to be candid and tell you the whole truth keeping nothing back. I will write you again tomorrow night & in the meantime if we fight, I hope through the blessings of an all wise God to be able to record a glorious victory for our army. One of the boys rec'd a letter stating that Pa will start to Savannah tomorrow. Goodby this time darling. Excuse a hurriedly written letter and believe that I am yours _ Fondly & Forever your Husband MBE

PS You must excuse franking this letter _ I will get some stamps as soon as I can Goodbye

Beaulieu, undated [around March 3, 1863; pages missing]

several ~~men~~ companies in our regiment-with nearly a hundred rank and file report about a dozen men for duty. My dear I wrote you in my last letter about the fight at Genesis Point at the mouth of the Ogeechee river I learned that the Yankees in that brush were repulsed & drew off; but ~~on yester~~ this morning at three o'clock they renewed their bombardment on ~~the~~ Fort McAlister.[5] I heard the cannon very distinctly. I am anxious to hear the result. If they should succeed in reducing the fort, they will pass up the River and destroy the steamer Nashville (provided she is not previous burned by the "rebels") They will also destroy the railroad bridge across the Ogeechee river. Our regiment – at least the remnant of well men may be sent down to stop them in their wild career – provided they should try to land - & by the way if we are sent they will get fits generally. My love, you spoke of sending a box of fruit to me. All right my love I'll thank you most heartily for them- Send by freight and do not pay – I can get ~~them~~ the box for nothing. My dear I am very glad that you have succeeded in getting some wool. I suppose the vest will not be amiss. I do not want any more woolen shirts. Bro J sent me seven military buttons. I shall write to George and get the buttons on that coat he carried off with him. I'll send them to you before you need them. We are prohibited from going to Savannah under any and all circumstances.

---

[5] In 1861, the Confederates built Fort McAllister, an earthen work fort at Genesis Point, at the mouth of the Ogeechee for defense of Union Naval attacks. It sustained seven attacks from various ironclads, but didn't fall until Sherman sent troops to attack it from land in December 1864. The fort fell in fifteen minutes. In an 1863 letter, Marcus spoke of the attack on the fort. The Savannah Republican reported that a number of tents were knocked down, but beyond that no damage was sustained. Until its fall, the fort protected the rice plantations that supplied the Confederate army and the Savannah, Albany, and Gulf Railroad, a vital supply line. "Attack on Fort McAllister," *Daily Constitutionalist* (Augusta GA), 4 March 1863, 3.

Glad of it, don't want to go – no use – save my money & c__ An arrangement has been made to furlough 6 or 8 men at a time. I shall take my turn in a month. Write soon my darling kiss the children Love to all – I will send some papers soon.

Yours forever, MBE

March 8, 1863

My Darling Wife,

Your very precious letter was received this evening & while I rejoiced at the privilege of hearing from you again, I could not but feel a little disappointment to think that we were separated by an additional number of miles. Besides the mail facilities are not so good. But I trust you will write by every mail & I will do the same. My dear Pa left Savannah on Friday evening, hence I suppose you met him in Macon. He did not stay with us but a very short time. He seemed to be very much pleased. However he can speak for himself in that particular. We have just heard of Van Dorn's splendid success in Tennessee – We have also learned that the Yanks have been repulsed at Vicksburg with a loss of three of their ironclads. But this report has not yet been confirmed though I do hope it is all true – The Yankee fleet off Beaulieu has disappeared to parts unknown. The Yanks still threaten in their papers to attack Savannah but we at present see no indications to point to an attack. It is believed by a good many there will be no fight here – If however they want to get into trouble this is the place to find it [rest of letter missing]

Beaulieu, March 10, 1863

My Dearest Love,

I was almost certain of receiving a letter by this evening's mail but I did not. I have just got up out of the bed – think I had a chill yesterday feel somewhat indisposed but nothing serious I hope. Hope you and the children reached home safely. Lt Brewster left for Harris this morning -

he did not say one word to me about it and of course I did not know he was going until he was gone – therefore I could not send you a note – not even a message, I shall take note of that little item – Don't think I'll forget it soon Besides the commander of the Regt. (Maj. Mann) knew nothing of it for I heard him say he was not consulted. He got leave of absence I suppose from some other source. No news to write – no prospect of a fight - the Yanks have left our vicinity for parts unknown. Our Regiment together with Harrison's, William's, First Ga State Troops & McHenry's battalion have been put in a brigade under Gen Taliferro.[6] Gen T is a Virginian and a good soldier. My dear you must look over a short note & write often I have not received a letter from you in several days. Write a long letter & tell me everything about home when furloughs resume I will come out.

Your affectionate Husband MBE

Beaulieu, March 17, 1863

My Dearest Wife

I was quite disappointed this evening when I ascertained there was no letter for me. It has been nearly two weeks since you left Forsyth and during all that time only one letter. I do not charge you with neglect my love, I am sure you do the best in your power. I am aware that the mails are only triweekly and chances rather slim to get your letters off to the post office. But never the less I want you to write often & when you do the very best you possibly can then I shall be as well satisfied under the circumstances as I possibly can be. I believe my dear I have no war news. Everything is remarkably still and quiet. Yet we do not slacken our energies because the enemy for a season have taken their departure. We are as busy preparing for them as if they were threatening us at every point. You learn from sending the papers they contemplated attacking

---

[6] General William Booth Taliaferro commanded troops in the Charleston area and briefly in Savannah in 1863. Boatner, *The Civil War Dictionary*, 825–26.

Charleston on or about the 20th inst. But whether they will make the attack on Charleston or draw off and attack some other point, time alone will determine. General Beauregard is on the alert at all times and will be ready to give the dastardly rascals a warm & bloody reception. I believe my love, the best news I have to impart is the Furloughs have been resumed, Lt. Bedell is entitled to the next leave of absence from our company but he has kindly given way to me. I shall therefore apply for a furlough as soon as Lt. Brewster returns. If there are no threatening disruptions on the coast for the next week I shall be able to get off without any difficulty. Two privates are also allowed to be absent from the company. I have been trying to make arrangements for Judson to get home. At this time however it is impossible for any of our men to leave as we have three or four absent without leave. When they return, two men can go home. If Pa will write to "Charlie"[7] and ask him to give Judson the first Furlough, I think he will as Judson has not been home in over a year. Dickson ought to go too, as I understand his sister is in Columbus. My dear if I am disappointed I shall let you know & it will be time enough to send you some money. I am glad Lizzie is going to school ~ at least that there is a prospect of her going. The coat you spoke of belongs to Sergeant Clay McCoy.[8] Write immediately I was on guard yesterday wasn't nearly all night excuse short letter. Love to all hope to see you soon,

Your affectionate Husband, MBE

---

[7] "Charlie" was Captain Charles R. Russell. Russell had a unique relationship with Osborn Ely. Charles's father died in 1851. Osborn was named as his guardian by the Muscogee Court of the Ordinary in 1851 and managed his financial affairs until he reached adulthood. *Muscogee County, GA Court of the Ordinary Minutes,* 351.

[8] Clay McCoy was a resident of Muscogee County and a 5th Sergeant in the Russell Guards. Henderson, *Roster of the Confederate Soldiers,* 5:700.

Pine Woods, March 22, 1863

Precious Husband,

The anticipated letter came to hand this morning ah! how glad was I to hear from your dear self once more. It really seems you grow more precious to me every day we live. I do not want to idolize you no, heaven forbid, a thing so sinful in the sight of God! Darling you must think I have just got into a good streak well be it so, the streak holds out a long time and seems rather to increase in strength as it grows, but enough of this, you ought to know my feelings as we have been living together for nearly eight years during which time our separation has been of short duration. Oh, my! if ever we could form a happy reunion now and never to be severed. Darling, you scold a little in your last letter or rather left me to think you were in doubt as to whether I did my best to get you letters regularly, let me here assure you my love I have done all in my power to promote a regular correspondence and further more I am never so well satisfied as when writing to you or perusing your dear letters and in fact this is the only pleasure I have when absent from you. My dear, this is the fourth letter I have written you since I left Forsyth and still you have received but one, there must be some right-down rascality – somewhere. I wish that I could detect the villainy. love, I will mail this letter in Columbus perhaps you may get it, hope so at least. I mailed you a letter in Columbus just one week since, that is I sent several to be mailed. Love you did not say anything about your chills hence I am led to hope they have left would it more for all time to come. I think you ought to resign if there be any chance of a resignation being, except I don't think I am disposed to complain. I know it might be much more with us, than it is now. I am glad that Dr. B has given his leave of absence to you, Dr. B will leave in a few days and then joy of joys!! You can come home again! Love, I have a nice lot of butter, was expecting to send it by Dr. B – but don't think I shall as you are coming. I may send a little and reserve the balance until you come up. If you should leave camp soon after Lt. B arrives you will not want the butter I send you though I guess you can find a ready mark for all that you don't want. Butter is selling for one dollar twenty cents in Columbus – did we ever think things would come to such a pass. Mary is well enough to be out. I have not succeeded in hiring her and brother thinks the chances rather slim. I wish Pa had consented for me to farm. I know he thought he was advising me for the best but I fear he is mistaken. Mr. Stribbin was buried today Sunday – Lizzie is going to school and I think learning very fast. I intend her to go regularly. She and Fannie[9] are in the same class. love, I must close as George will leave soon and I intend sending this letter by him. I received a letter from Mrs. Mercer will answer it in a few days. I think her a splendid lady and a worthy correspondent. Good bye darling. I will write by Dr. B when he returns to camp. Your devoted wife Mattie Ely

Love, I dreamed of you last night what a vision of bliss you had been out on a fishing expedition and returned with your spoils – two splendid sea fish – such as I have never seen. Your precious face was bright with a glow of satisfaction. I dislike to stop but I have finished the sheet.

Beaulieu, March 29, 1863

My dearest love,

I wrote you a short "turbulent" note by Capt Russell, being troubled at the time I wrote it. Since then, I have received two letters from you, which gave me infinite pleasure. I am now well satisfied that I do not receive more than half of your letters. There is a great mystery somewhere but I cannot unravel it. My darling I just had my furlough sent back disapproved. I am very much disconcerted about it. When there is so much difference shown between officers I become somewhat disgusted and my patriotism oozes out at the ends of my fingers. If Lt Bedell returned promptly I would have had no difficulty in getting my

[9] Fannie Ely was Marcus's half-sister, the daughter of Osborn and Jane Russell Ely. *1860 U.S. Federal Census, Georgia, Muscogee County*, 351.

furlough. When it was up, Gen Talifero referred to the report and found Lt B reported without case _hence my furlough came back disapproved. Therefore the subject will be dismissed for there is no probability of getting off. In fact Brewster is still absent & no one knows when he will return for he sent word by Mrs. McLeroy that we need not look for him until we saw him. My love it is Saturday night although I have dated my letter for tomorrow~ hence I cannot go to Savannah till Monday am afraid my butter will not be in good condition_ I am very glad you sent it_ though we are tolerably well so far as getting something to eat is concerned. We have plenty of oysters_ also potatoes which we get for the moderate sum of $4.00 per bushel – We have also some eggs on hand – only 75 cts per doz. We can get hams for $1.00 per pound. Don't you consider it a great "luxury" to be an officer in the confederate army? Capt Burke our Qtrmaster said that a private was better off ~than an officer which seems unreasonable to some but it is just as true as Paul's epistle to the Romans. It is true a private gets but little but his wants are few as he has all his clothing, food, shoes, caps ~ everything furnished whereas an officer has to furnish everything. If he wants a suit of clothing they will cost him two months wages (160.00) (I speak of a Lts. Pay) A pair of boots will cost him $50.00 over half a month's pay cap $20.00) ¼ months pay Sword $40.00 Overcoat $60.00__ Shirts &c&c 50.00. Besides his transportation on Railroad__hire of cook_cost of provisions _tobacco_ and a thousand and one incidental expenses which will amount to over a thousand dollars in six months when his salary is but little over that for a year. If Congress does not raise the pay of the Officer, they can not live without stealing or begging. I have thus been particular in making these statements to ____________ the minds of a great many persons who think an officer getting $80.00 or $100.00 per month was making an independent fortune. My love I suppose you think I am running out of soap~ well I am just that~ I have nothing else to write about; everything is awful dull ~ nothing breaks the monotony ~ one day will be as a sample for a week ~ only we do sometimes have sunshine ~ sometimes a little rain – sometimes a calm ~ sometimes a gale ~ I have had my days of chills my love but still am not very well. I have a pain in my heart __

_________ ______ think it is caused from a diseased state of my liver. I become bilious every few days and am obliged to take medicine - still I am getting on tolerably well. I was very sorry to hear of Millin Thornton. He and poor Billie McLeroy have gone the way of all the earth & and had it not been for this war both of them would be alive and well today. But our troubles have scarcely begun – There is not half as much prospect of a termination of this war as there was on the day that Fort Sumpter was reduced. All the nations of the earth have forsaken us and turned their cold shoulder ~ The north is in terrible earnest in the prosecution of the war to enslave us. The north western troubles have all calmed down - Intervention the great humbug has played out _ and if God almighty forsakes us we are gone suckers. I believe there is no news ~ You get the papers and see what is transferring _ Two Yankee Captains, one privateer & a large mail together with 6 gals of brandy were taken prisoners a few days since just above us. I reckon our men paroled a portion of the brandy. I read some of their letters – quite indecent – but just as we would expect of a depraved people – I also saw the New York news 17th inst _ There are 150 vessels off Port Royal – that they will attack Charleston. I will go up town on Monday, will express you some money & write again.

Love to all Your devoted Husband MBE

Undated [March 1863?]

My dear I have written about all the news I hope that furloughs will be resumed soon & that I can get to come home. If you have fixed up that suit for which I gave you the buttons you will please send it to me. I intend to keep it for services & inspections. Also my boots at Mr. McLeroys as I am nearly barefooted. My dear we have plenty to eat at present Pa brought down a whole barrel of provisions. I tell you I hated to see him leave – I was sorry he could not stay a week with us. I tried to make him as comfortable as possible. My love write as often as you can Goodbye my love

Your affectionate Husband MBE

PS I wrote by this mail to your brother James enclosing him ten dollars let me know when you write how much money you need and I will send it to you immediately

Yours MBE

Beaulieu, April 1, 1863, 9 o'clock

My Darling Mattie,

I met the mail this evening with the expectation of getting a letter from you but was disappointed. I shall not complain, however, as I have received two letters from you in the last five days. I wrote you on Monday last enclosing a check for forty dollars which you will give to Pa and he will get the money at the Express Office in Columbus Lt Brewster is still absent. He is in Savannah, but I learn that he will not join our company under thirty days. I do not know what he means by staying away. He may be sick but I imagine he is making one last desperate effort to get out of service. It is a great pity he is such a specimen of humanity, otherwise he might get out of service on Surgeon's Certificate of disability Well love it seems my game is blocked No chance for me to get off. Russell gone -Brewster gone. Bedell gone to Savannah and for the present I am shouldering all the responsibility. My chances of getting a furlough when I was a private were much better than they are now. Under the existing circumstances I have concluded that I cannot get off home~ I can stay where I am. I have therefore provided myself with some letter paper ($2.80 quire)[10] Some envelopes $1.25 per pack & steel pens (10 cts each) and am now ready to mail letters to you in the shortest order if not in the most approved style. Everything is about Status quo ~ about Beaulieu. We have no war news ~ It is believed by some that the storm is gathering at Charleston and that it will soon burst in all its fury upon that devoted city. But the Federals have deceived us so much heretofore in regard to their moves that it is hard to

[10] Quire was a term for a set of 24 to 25 pages of paper of the same size and stock. Guralnik, *New World Dictionary,* 1167.

determine anything in regard to their intended movements on the coast. The French Consul having left Charleston is regarded by some as a sure omen that the attack is close at hand. If they intend to try their mettle either against Charleston or Savannah the sooner the better for me as I am tired of this suspense.[11] Both cities are in a complete state of defense & I have no idea that they will be any better prepared for the Federals in the future than they are at present. Much depends upon the fate of these two cities. If they fall ~ the war will be protracted. Otherwise a failure may have a tendency to shorten it. "Nous verrou" In one of your letters love you asked if I were still having chills. I have been troubled with them recently. In fact my health at present is very good. I have been naming tacktics till I have nearly addled my brain. I will say "file right"~ file left right about to my horse in plowing instead of saying gee haw Love my shoes are too large they scarcely stay on my feet. I shall keep them for winter& wear two pairs of socks. Found my butter all right. Will fare well as long as it lasts. Am very thankful to you for your kindness. Love, I wish to speak about Lizzie & her going to school &c at any note you will see Miss McEntire and particularly request her not to confine Lizzie in the school room but to let her roam at large & if she does not learn no blame will be attached to anybody. I want you to put Eddy to learning his multiplication tables and advise me occasionally as to his progress. My candle is flickering in its socket. My ideas are exhausted ~ my eyes are heavy for want of sleep. Good night darling dear

Love to all

Your affectionate and Devoted Husband MBE

---

[11] The *Macon Telegraph* reported that members of the French Consul were departing earlier than expected on the French man-of-war Catinat. It is rumored they had heard of an imminent attack on Charleston by Union forces and made haste to leave American shores. France never recognized the Confederate States of America. "Departure of the French Consul at Charleston," *Macon* (GA) *Telegraph*, 4 April 1863, 1.

Beaulieu, April 8, 1863

My Precious Wife,

Your very kind letter date 6th inst was received on the 7th the quickest trip on record. Of course I was mighty glad to hear from you and to know you were well &c. I wrote you a long letter a few days ago ~ This will not be so lengthy as my time is somewhat limited at present. You gave me a very extensive programme to pursue all of which I may consider at some future period of my life. Glad to know Ed enjoys whittling and that Lizzie is making some progress at school ~ Sorry you do not mention the children often in your letters ~~ Dr Brewster's chills have returned. He went to Savannah this morning, where he will remain until he beats his chills. As to getting a furlough to come home that is entirely out of the question. In fact the campaign for the year is about to open & furloughs may not resume at all. They are not granted under any circumstances. The enemy are threatening Charleston already. Several thousand troops around Savannah have gone onto participate in the fight. We will not go unless Gen Beauregard finds the enemy too strong. The Examining Board convenes tomorrow. I am tolerable well prepared posted. Lt Bedell is ordered before it again also about a dozen other officers. Lem says he will take 1500 Dollars for his place. If I can make arrangements I will give him his price. I shall write to Pa by this mail. Brother James & Judson are quite well. Jimmy is in very good health. He sends love to you and all the family. Send me some eggs if you can get them my dear. I sold one cake of butter for $11.25 and have plenty to last a month besides dividing with Jimmy & Judson.

Your Devoted Husband

Beaulieu, April 8, 1863

My Darling Wife I congratulate myself that I have an opportunity of sending you a letter direct by Mr. Raley. As I wrote you by mail on yesterday of course you cannot expect much news. The ball is opened at Charleston. On yesterday the Iron clads opened on the forts and today it is reported the ironclad Keokuk[12] was sunk off Morris Island. But you will get all the details in the papers. I send a pipe to Pa. It was made by a private in our regiment, I hope he will like it. I also enclose him $20.00 a revolutionary relic. It is a great curiosity and will give one an idea what kind of money our forefathers had. It is dated 1778 just 85 years ago. The Palmetto necklace[13] is a present to daughter. She must wear it to school. You must send me a letter by Raley when he returns. But love as he will not return until the expiration of ten days ~~ you must write at least three or four times before that time. I see no prospect of getting off. In fact no furloughs are granted. Raley is a teamster & that is the reason he got off. Mrs. Stribling is coming down. John Stribling[14] is the most consummate jack-ass that ever brayed, McC has written his wife [John's] bright smiles – a love sick – of so sickening ~~ The letter was intercepted still it went on to its destination. Now let me enjoin you not to let this thing get out as it will cause a fuss. Read this letter burn it & nobody will be the wiser.

Love to all Your devoted Husband MBE

---

[12] The USS Keokuk was a Union ironclad ship involved in an attack on Charleston, South Carolina on April 7, 1863. The Keokuk sailed into the Charleston harbor ahead of a large flotilla of ironclads. But, weather and other unfortunate circumstances caught the Keokuk in the harbor where it was bombarded for several hours by Confederate forces. It sunk off Morris Island early the next morning. According to several newspaper accounts, thirteen men were wounded during the attack; two were expected to die. "'Terrible Slaughter' on Board the Keokuk," *Daily Constitutionalist* (Augusta GA), 10 April 1863, 1.

[13] Palmetto leaves were used for weaving clothing such as hats. Boiled and dried leaves were also used to make pillows and mattresses. Many of the soldiers on the coast wore palmetto hats to ward off the effects of summer heat. Kelby Ouchey, *Flora and Fauna of the Civil War: An Environmental Reference Guide* (New Orleans LA: Louisiana State University, 2010) 72.

[14] John Stribling was a private in the Russell Guards and a neighbor of the Ely family (see Co. H 54th "The Russell Guards" Biographies). *1860 U.S. Federal Census, Georgia, Harris County*, 88.

Beaulieu, April 12, 1863

My Darling Wife

I have the pleasure of devoting a portion of this beautiful Sabbath evening to writing you a short letter. Jack Walker[15] will leave for home tomorrow and you may be able to get the letter sent through him earlier than by mail. Darling I wrote to you on yesterday & last night I received your letter It was a source of great pleasure to me, wish I could hear from you every day. There is nothing more cheering to a soldier in camp than a fond missile of love from his dear loving wife far away. Love I have nothing interesting to write. It was rumored on yesterday that the enemy would renew the attack on Charleston today by land and water. It is also stated that a large force of Confederate troops from Virginia have arrived, enough to swell our army at Charleston to 5,000 men. I think our forces at Charleston will come out victorious for I have no idea they have ever for one moment contemplate a defeat. I wish it were all over. For when everything settles down to a calm ~~ I may be able to get off home. At present no one can leave except they have a sick family at home or have other extreme case of a similar nature. I shall go down to Montgomery soon & see if I can make an arrangement to get a room in the Bakersly house. I will let you know love in my next what the prospects are. Our tents are full of women. Mrs. Tarvin, Mrs. McLeroy, Mrs.Kendrick, Mrs. Brown_ Railey &c and others coming. We will soon be able to organize an army of women in our Regiment~ There are also a great many children, dogs, fleas, sand flies &c&c&c The boys are catching plenty of mullet now You should be here to eat fish. I must close this imperfect note Hope you'll get it soon & I will write again in two or three days You need not be surprised to hear from me by almost every mail.

Love to all Your affectionate Husband MBE I am well all but a cold

---

[15] John J. "Jack" Walker was a member of the Russell Guards (see Co. H 54th "The Russell Guards" Biographies). Henderson, *Roster of the Confederate Soldiers,* 5:700.

Beaulieu, April 13, 1863

My Darling Wife

I wrote to you yesterday by Jack Walker but as there is no certainty that you will get the letter soon I will write again. You perceive I am very punctual love in writing _ and I hope you receive all my letters punctually. Well love I was drawn up before the Military Board today. I came out all right_, did not miss a single question The Col came to me after the examination and told me that I had passed & would not have to go before the board any more. This then is my first and last time. Bedell went up, today for the third time and I learn that he passed after so long a time. Lt. Brewster is still absent _ in Savannah though I understand he will be down tomorrow. Bedell is on a court martial _ and I am in command of the company. I am getting very tired of acting Captain and getting Lieutenant's pay Besides it is very confining, for while there is but one Officer in Command of the Company he has to stay there all the time. ~~~ Abe McLeroy's[16] wife's child is quite sick It had a spasm this evening. I have no more news~ Everything about Beaulieu is as still as a "mice." I begin to have some faint hopes that this war will not last always. Whenever the North is fully convinced that the subjugation of the South is utterly impossible they will make peace and I think from the signs of the times, that the truth is forcing itself on them now. I shall try again to get home in a few days can not say how I'll succeed. The Commissary and the Corporal (Jimmy & Judson) are well.

Write often Love to all Your Affectionate Husband MBE

[5th page]

My dear, of course you must bring Eddie with you; if you leave him there will be a fuss kicked up on his part. You can give Lizzie to her Grandpa at least for awhile – that she may continue at school. My dear I

---

[16] Abraham McLeroy was a resident of Harris County and a neighbor of Osborn Ely. He was a member of the Russell Guards (see Co. H 54th "The Russell Guards" Biographies). *1860 U.S. Federal Census, Georgia, Harris County*, 581.

am threadbare almost naked. I want some cotton socks ~ also some summer clothing. The weather is getting very warm. You may also bring me a white shirt, also my felt hat and a summer vest. I do trust my love that I shall be able to get off next week. Then you know ~~I can~~ you and Maggy can come back ~~as~~ when I do. I shall not apply but for a week. You will be obliged to have a little negro, I suppose Pa can supply you with one. One will do for you and Sister both if she comes. If I do not get home and you come with out me – don't forget my meerschaum pipe & let us know what day you will reach Savannah. Love to all both, white and "cullod" I must quit writing ~ shake a few fleas off and go to bed.

I am darling yours as ever & ever MBE

Beaulieu, April 15, 1863

My Darling wife,

Your letter of the 12th inst was received this evening and nothing short of your presence at Beaulieu could have received a warmer welcome. It is very strange that I get your letters in two days after they are written & you do not get mine in a week or ten days after they are written. The fault lies in the P.O. in Columbus ~~ Look Out! They will get a decent "ribbing" before long through the papers. I write three or four letters every week but I have an idea you receive more than half of them. You advise me not to buy John. Of course I had no idea of making the trade without Pa's consent. Jimmy told me he would take $1500 for him. My reply was __ "I will give it to you if Pa is willing and will sell him and divide the profits." I could have sold him for $2000, but without Pa's consent I would not have purchased him, if I could have sold him on the spot for $5000 You said something about clothing ~~ I am scarce but can make out for the present One pr of my pants have failed. When Russell gets back next week I shall try to get a leave of absence for a few days so you need not send me any thing except a long letter. You said something about sending a tobacco pouch. I will take the will for the deed my darling. I would not give a straw for all the pouches in the Confederacy. All that I said in a previous letter to sister about tobacco pouches was meant for a joke and I am very sorry. She misconstrued it

Tell eddie he must get on the cars and come down to see his Pa. Tell Sister she must learn to write so she can write her Pa a letter. Write by Railey once and as often as you can

Your Aff Husb MBE

Tuesday night, April 28, 1863

My Dearest Love,

Your affectionate letter was received this evening, met with the warmest reception and in fact nothing else save your precious self could have found half the welcome. Darling I received a long letter from you on Saturday and answered it the first thing on Sunday but have not yet had the opportunity of mailing it. I will however send it in the same envelope with some items in it that I do not wish to respond to again. Love, you must come home if you can get off. For, I don't believe I will get to Columbus if you are not here to help me off and besides our business demands your immediate attention. I don't know how things may go at Perry if we don't have the will proven soon. We may use our interest entirely. Love, I will make an effort to get Aunt Leasie from Mr. Hightower. She would suit very well to take along. Could do all of our washing &c. Leasie and Mary[17] were here Sunday last. Leasie says Mr. Hightower is very unkind to her and pushes her very hard – makes her work in the rain – She has a very bad cough. Pa will go over to his house in a few days – I don't know what will be the result of his trip. Hightower has not given his note yet. Perhaps he may let her off. I don't think he will have it as a resale. I let him have the negro for a "mere song" with conditions understood which were as follows: no working in bad weather and not hard labor any time, both of which he has violated

---

[17] Aunt Leasie and Mary were slaves belonging to Marcus and Mattie Ely. Mary would later be sent to Savannah to work in the Bethesda Military Hospital. Records of Mary Ely were filed along with Marcus Ely (her story can be found in People and Places). National Archives, *Compiled Service Records from Georgia Units, Catalog ID 586957, 54th Infantry, Marcus B. Ely*, 1863.

and I am determined to get her away if I can get her. If Pa fails to get her I want you to try when you come home. If we had Aunt Leasie with us she could make something by washing – I don't think there will be any chance for us to get a little negro at Pa's – I would not ask him for the whole value of one. Love, I heard this morning that Bill Hart's wife is very low, but I don't know how to credit the report as you said nothing about it in your letter. I should think it right bad for her to be sick in camp. Love we have just had a most delightful rain, the first one in a long time. I guess Mr. Buce will be home tomorrow- would be extremely happy for you to come with him. I shall look for you in all events – hope I shall not look in vain. Love – I wish you could see what a light I have penned this letter by the poorest kind of pine light. I can scarcely see what I am doing, don't think you will be able to read it – half candles are scarce about this place and I got your letter too late this evening to answer it by daylight. yes dear I will be able to carry Edd and don't know but it be better for Lizzie to go too as she is too young to leave so long – She wants to go with us – says she is tired of going to school – I don't expect she will learn much if we leave her and then she might get sick and we would not hear from her – I have been thinking it all over and trying to get my consent to leave our little daughter behind – but my heart – don't see a "merry time" – however we will discuss the subject at a future time when we have a brighter light and a better pen than upon this occasion. The small pox is pretty much the same – no new cases – and the only one is getting well – The families who have been exposed keep themselves quarantined. Well love I know that you are tired with reading this shabby epistle. Nothing new or strange has occurred of late – I hope this ____ ____ scroll will meet you in Columbus tomorrow evening.

Good night my darling, your loving wife, Mattie F. Ely

Myself and the children are well except colds

Beaulieu, April 19, 1863

My Darling Wife

I have just learned that Mrs. McLeroy will start home in the morning and I will avail myself of the opportunity of writing you a note. I was glad to hear from you through Mrs. Brewster – but was disappointed in not getting a letter from you. I suppose though you must have had a good excuse for not writing. I have not rec'd but one letter this week from you. I am almost certain you would have written but the mail as usual is out of gear. Lt. Brewster is in Savannah with his wife. This makes the second night of his absence. It seems that all of them can take more latitude than I can. I have not been two hundred yards from the camp limits in three weeks ~~ except when I was on Picket at the Battery. I am getting very tired of the confinement in camp. Way, Mann, Lt Brewster, Adjt. Brantley and myself are endeavoring to rent one of those large houses in Montgomery. Lt B will return probably tomorrow or next day and report whether or not we can get a house. Mrs. Brewster will return to Harris next Tues or Wednesday __ If Charles Russell gets back at the expiration of his leave of absence I may get off (provided I get my furlough approved) about the time Mrs. B returns ~~I haven't a word of news ~~ went a fishing this evening ~~ no success whatever the tattoo beats, I must close and attend roll call You must look over a short letter this time Good by my little darling

Yours Devotedly MBE

Beaulieu, April 21, 1863

My Darling Wife

I was delighted to receive your long letter from Railey on yesterday. I was glad to hear from you love ~~ was sorry you had such a cold _ but hope you are ere this as bright as a new pin. You wrote me a charmingly long and interesting letter love, and of course I will reciprocate. So far as length is concerned, but whether it be of much interest or not, I will let you decide. I suppose Mrs. Maggie B. had reached home and given you all the dots. She has probably informed you that we have rented the

Foreman house at Montgomery for the reception of our families _ I should have mentioned that Maj Mann __ Adjt B__Lt. B & myself (with our families) will constitute the occupants of the Foreman mansion. We pay $10.00 per month each for the privilege of using all the furniture. The house is three stories high – has eight or ten comfortable rooms _ There are plenty of chairs tables wash stands, pitchers & bedsteads bureaus _wardrobes and in fact almost anything you can think of or imagine. I suppose you have seen the house It is next to Capt Newells. It is a most enchanting spot _ the yard is full of the most delicious sweet smelling flowers and among them none more fragrant than the honeysuckle and the _____ We can have a delightful time sailing fishing bathing &c There is a splendid bath house attached to the place which will need a few slight repairs to make it all right. If I do not get off when Russell comes, I want you to come down with Mrs. Brewster. Tell Sister I have a nice little room attached to ours __ with bureau & a nice bedstead & mattress which I have reserved for her. She would be perfectly delighted __ yes enchanted with the extreme loveliness of our house on the banks of the Vernon River. I send an inventory of such articles as we will need which will be furnished by all the parties. Besides we hire a cook from Regt ~~ Old Chance~~ He is the best cook in the Confederacy. Love the fleas bite so I can hardly write a word They are awful tonight ~ I write a word or two and then stop to scratch. Gen Talifero reviewed the regiment today. It was a very pretty spectacle. We serenaded him last night at the Battery. The old fellow invited us in the house and thanked us for the music. He is accompanied with several aides among them several Virginians. I took five of our men & went scouting yesterday on Skidaway Island. I went to the eastern part of the island where no one has been in more than a year. The Yankees are on the island very frequently I could see where they had written on the walls of all the houses I visited. On one of the houses five Yanks had written their names & stated that they belonged to the _______ "Storm Bird" One Yank wrote his name on the wall & wrote that he belonged to the 158th New York Regt. We saw some cattle & hogs __ shot a hog in tolerable good _____ but being full of lice we concluded not to eat him. Well dear I want you to get ready to come down as soon as possible & if Sister wants to come let her to come along. I shall write again in two or three days & then I can let you know whether I can come home or not. I am anxious to come home on account of some pressing business matter. Billy Brown went home yesterday to see his "Kitten"!!!~~I can hear him in my imagination talking ~~Why –S-Sallie bless your little soul. Billy's & Sallie's baby is a girl only a few days old. My love I forgot to say you must bring a pillow – two sheets – pillow slips & one bed quilt also some eggs & butter if you can get it

[Last part missing]

Beaulieu, April 24, 1863

My Darling wife

I received your very dear letter on yesterday evening and I was "monstrous" glad indeed to have the exquisite pleasure of perusing another letter from you. I wrote you a long letter on day before yesterday, informing you of our success in renting a large and as well as partly furnished house in Montgomery We are all very proud of our house. Maj Mann carries the keys ~ We go down nearly every day to inspect the premises. We will have the bathing house fixed up by the time you come down. I shall carry a large boat down tomorrow for us to sail in every evening. Lt B has just rec'd a letter from Mrs B. He says he cannot see to write tonight – will write tomorrow. I suppose you and Mrs B have talked and "retalked" over your trip to Montgomery. My love I shall apply for a week's leave as I have some important business ~ You must perfect all you arrangements and if I am not there by the first of May you may conclude I failed to get off & not wait for me any longer but start next Friday or Monday following. You must get Pa to let you have Mary or some of the little negroes to wait on you If Sister comes she must bring a few bed clothing, pillow &c I have a nice little bedstead and mattress for her Have also selected her a nice room joining ours. Tell Sister I am much obliged for the tobacco pouch ~ but I cannot get any tobacco to put in it. We look for Russell tomorrow he has been absent without leave several days. If he had returned to camp as he should have done I might have been home now. I have not been absent from camp but eight days in nearly six months...

[Rest of letter missing]

Beaulieu, December 22, 1863

My Darling Wife

I reached camp last night a 11 o'ck – left Columbus at 7 ¾ o'clock Sunday pm. I did not make any stop at Ft Valley as Mr. McCoy's son was with me & besides I felt anxious to get to camp. All were very much surprised to see me back – so soon in fact when I counted up I found that my furlough did not expire until after Christmas. I am very sorry I did not stay a week longer. I regret it exceedingly, but it can not be remedied now. Now for the news ~ Dr. Brewster has been released from the Barracks & is now a private in Co. H. Sure enough as was rumored. Capt. Russell is being court martialed about that Government cloth. I suppose he will be acquitted. Capt. Hanleiter has reduced his orderly sergeant for cursing him & has given him lodging in the Bomb proof. Lt Shaw had a street fight in Savannah with a Capt. Jackson, son of General Jackson. Jackson called him a coward & Shaw mounted him. Dr. B has tripped out to hard swearing. While in the Barracks Capt Russell asked him where he slighted ~ he pointed his finger to the floor & replied "Right down there with a parcel of thieves and cutthroats." My dear Dr. Houston wants to hire a woman to cook at the Bethesda Hospital. He offers $25.00 per month or $300.00 a year Besides she can get transportation to Savannah. If you think the arrangement a good one or not hire her. If I do not hire her to Dr. H I can make it profitable getting out oysters. They are worth $10.00 per gal and we have __________ all the boats ~ about 40 I have a very distressing cough otherwise I am tolerably well. The boys are back. Can you read this letter I think not Kiss my babys Write as often as possible

Your affectionate Husband MBE

In Camp, December 26, 1863

My Beloved Wife

I was looking this evening for a "Christmas Gift" from you, in the shape of a letter but it did not come. I know I will receive it in a day or two. Yesterday was Christmas ~ a very dull one indeed for me. In truth I was a little "homesick" My long stay at home has spoilt me & again it seems so unnatural to be from home during Christmas. I do most sincerely hope & trust that ere another Christmas rolls around we will be together & to past no more on earth. By the way we killed the black pullet & had a chicken pie yesterday for our Christmas dinner. No one made me any presents, but I found a "quarter" as I was going to the battery to sign the grand report, Don't you think I am lucky? My dear, Gen Mercer[18] has written to Gen Beauregard & influenced him to prohibit Dr. Brewster from going before the board at Charleston, hence Dr. B will be compelled to remain a private in Co. H. Dr. Brewster is the most reckless man you ever saw. Capt Russell says he acts like a person going deranged. His profanity would shock you. In fact it seems very strange to hear him cursing & swearing about the camp. My love you must not let these facts get out in the neighborhood. If his wife hears of it__ let her hear it from some other source. I do not wish to get the reputation of a "news carrier." If you wish to hire Mary to the hospital send her down I will send you some money soon. Please send my sash by the first one passing. You know I forgot it. I learn there is a Yankee Fleet at Ft. Pulaski. Do not know what they are after. Tell Cousin Fannie, Dick has gone back to Charleston ~ gave the tobacco bag to the Captain, Jimmy & Jud are well pleased with theirs. My cough is not so distressing as it has been. Love to all Kiss the children. Trust you are spending a Merry Christmas & I heartily wish you darling a happy New Year

Devotedly MBE

---

[18] General Hugh Weedon Mercer commanded the post of Savannah for most of the war (see People and Places). Boatner, *The Civil War Dictionary*, 542–43.

1864

"I Know You Will Cherish My Memory"

Beaulieu, January 5, 1864, dated 13th inst

My Precious Darling

I have just returned from Savannah and am very much fatigued hence I shall not write a very voluminous epistle. I had the exquisite happiness of receiving your very dear letter today & though of ancient date (28th Dec) yet it afforded me an infinite amount of pleasure. Yes darling I was indeed delighted to read those precious lines full of devotion & affection from my dear dear wife my joy my all. Love I expressed to you today $100.00 which you will get by applying to the Express Office Columbus, GA. Tomorrow I will send up a jug of oysters for you and Pa & also to the rest if they love them. I will send up a box in a few days containing Palmetto & other things. My love you may send Mary & Leasie down to our camp. I can get 50 or 60 dollars for the two. Strawbridge[1] ~~will be~~ has gone home on furlough He will return on Thursday 14th. He has kindly consented to take charge of these negroes & bring them to the camp I shall write again & send transportation for Mary provided I make or rather perfect the trade. Darling I wrote a few lines to Pa. I hope he has become better reconciled I must write to Sister. Oh! how I want to see you my darling & the children. Do write often This is the fifth letter I have written to you Good night darling I must stop my light is out

Your Devoted Husband MBEly

---

[1] W. B. Strawbridge was a resident of Harris County and a member of the Russell Guards. Henderson, *Roster of the Confederate Soldiers*, 5:708.

Cataula, January 15, 1864

My Precious Husband,

Your precious letter of the 15th was received this evening and you can't imagine how delighted I was to hear that your health was improving – but gracious knows I don't want you to get as fat as old Matthew Gibbs or at least I would not like for you to stand out before quite so much. I know you had a hard time during that cold weather thought of you often yes very often. I expected that you would have been down that old river freezing but we ought to be very glad that things are ever so well with us and you are not now in Tennessee or Virginia. Well darling I have nothing new to write, I can however confirm the rumor with regard to Mary Howard and Hanks, all true she did elope with him and no mistake, I would have mentioned it before this but thought everybody would be writing it sooner and it would be worn out completely. we have seen none of the family since the mighty event! But, presume everything is racking along smoothly. I heard Mrs. Park said she was much better satisfied than at first I don't know how _____ with her; she thinks with the old adage "what can't be done, must be endured." I sent down to know of Mr. Strawbridge when and where to meet him with the blacks and he sent me that he had been to Columbus and had his furlough extended to now. I don't know when he will leave, however he promised to let me know. Love though that you would send me transportation for Mary I don't know whether I must send her along without it & you wrote me that you would send it up you must have forgotten to do so and our express ____ too, what must we do about that? Can't get the money without Pa has not yet applied for it – as he has not been to Columbus, but I feel certain he could not get it without presenting a receipt, please do send it up if you have one. Pa has not been to Columbus since you left. Pa has employed a man to look after his business, an old man. Darling, I think I have a chance of getting some pork, from old Mr. Cox sale above Hamilton, the sale comes on the 27th of this month. If I succeed in getting this pork, I will keep house and therefore send you only Mary as I will need old Leasie to do my cooking. Pa wants me to open my school next Monday, I guess I shall both live and teach at the Stribbin house. I will propose for Pa to cultivate our little farm and make us ______ for next year. I will send Leasie if I fail getting the pork – Do not trouble about the palmetto yet, if you have it gathered – I think it will be better in the Spring________________ _________ have spoke to have you some butter saved and will send it by the first chance. I sent your sash and toothbrush by Mrs. Jones and also a letter. Now dear I must close as it is late Goodnight God bless you my precious Husband Your devoted wife Mattie Ely

All are well the children and myself have good health write long letters and tell me all your arrangements with whom you _____ and lodge &c Our babies are asleep or they would have a message for Papa

Camp near Beaulieu, January 17, 1864

My Darling Wife,

I am in receipt of two letters from you __ one through the mail – the other by Mrs. Railey – both reaching me about the same time hence all my happiness came in a heap. My love I was so overjoyed to receive your letters and I perused them with the greatest pleasure imaginable.

I am very sorry love, your mail accommodations are so poor. Do not let this matter trouble your mind. Write as often as you can and I shall be perfectly satisfied. You did not get my last in time enough to send Leasie & Mary down to _______ not. William Strawbridge did not leave at the time I specified in my letter. If you have made no disposition of them I hope you will send them along as soon as possible. I am sorry they are there to trouble and fret you. My love there has been some trouble around and about Beaulieu. Some of the troops at Rose Dew and at several other points have made a feeble attempt to mutineer. Troops were sent from Savannah to guard these affected fellows and the disturbance was quelled after several of the ring leaders were arrested. Dr. Brewster is Hospital steward at Bethesda. I think he has changed as he seems to be very quiet and orderly of late. I received a letter yesterday from Sallie Dumas. She enquired where to direct letter to you stating that she had written several directing them to Cataula, GA & had not heard from you. Your brother relapsed & was very sick but is convalescing. He sent a can to get some oysters but the Government has seized the Express Office & no private freight can be shipped. I expressed a box to you two or three days ago. You must get it as soon as possible as the palmetto may spoil. I sent 40 lbs. of rice for all of you to eat. You will find a pipe and tobacco for Pa. Let me know if Pa likes his pipe & stem which I fixed to it. John Massey[2] will make me another soon which I will send also. I will enclose the receipts but if you have not got the oysters they have spoiled. I have made $50.00 in the last ten days on oysters. I do not get wet I go with the boys. They fill my boat and get out one half for the other. I'll send you some money soon. I have commenced to read my Bible through. I read one or two chapters every day [unfinished]

Beaulieu, January 21, 1864

My Precious Wife,

Your "billet doux" or messenger of love dated 18th inst met with a warm and affectionate welcome & if you refer to date of my letter you will applaud my punctuality. I am very glad love you write so frequently for you know it is a soldier's chief solace to get letters from his dear wife. In regard to those negroes my love you may send them at once, Dr. Houston is getting very impatient. He has been waiting on me ever since the first of Jan. You can send them by express in care of the conductor. Let me know when you will send them that I make arrangements to meet them in Savannah provided you cannot send them under the protection of Strawbridge. My love you made some inquiries concerning my domestic arrangements. I mess with our officers. We have plenty to eat as several boxes have been received lately. We have a heavy expense to meet. We paid 79.00 for 10 lbs. lard 16 lbs sugar & 1 gal. molasses,

---

[2] John J. Massey lived in the Mountain Hill area of Harris County and was a member of the Russell Guards (see Co. H 54th "The Russell Guards" Biographies). *1860 U.S. Federal Census, Georgia, Harris County*, 96.

hence you see at once we make money fly. I am lodging at the present with Dr. Houston, or rather he is lodging with me. He has left his cottage on the seashore. The old fellow and I have a good time together. The better I find him out the more I admire his good qualities. In short, he is a noble old fellow. He sends his respects to you. I sent the express receipts several days ago in accordance with your request, however it was unnecessary as Pa can call and get anything directed to him without the receipts. I am afraid the oysters have spoiled although there was vinegar & salt in the jug.

I will send you about 100 or 150 dollars in about ten days. If you need anything that Confederate money will buy - don't short yourself. I hope you can get the pork. If you fail send __________ on - the butter, too provided you can get it. There is no news. We have a ten inch Columbiad weighing 15,000 lbs. mounted at Beaulieu Battery. It is a perfect sight. We are all well &send love & c. You must be satisfied this time love with a dull letter.

Write soon. Your devoted, MBEly

Beaulieu, January 23, 1864

My Darling Wife,

I received your "little small" letter this evening and was as usual overjoyed to hear from you my darling wife. I have written several letters recently- also sent by letter three receipts. Of course, I would not send anything by express without taking a receipt. And Pa could not get your money? Well, we will see about that. I will have the money rest assured of that fact. Take care of the receipt and present it at the Express Office in Columbus. Then, if the money is not forth with coming, mail it or send it back by someone to me and I will pull it out of these fellows at Savannah. I am sorry you have not received it before now. I will send you some more money next week and enclose a receipt also that you may get it immediately. However, receipts are unnecessary except to recover goods or packages when lost. As far as transportation is concerned that is out of the question. I cannot get transportation. You must pay her way.

Darling, not withstanding you complained a little. I write twice as many letters as I receive. In fact, I write 2 or 3 letters every week. I suppose you do not receive them all. You will receive a letter from me next Thursday, also one Saturday & Tuesday, the following. Mrs. B shall not receive more letters than Mrs. E. My love, send and get your Palmetto before it spoils & perhaps by that time your money will be there, the express is not paid on your box of palmetto. I will send you just as much money as you want.

Beaulieu, January 25, 1864

My Precious Wife,

As I am on duty tonight I shall not be able to write a very lengthy epistle Besides I expect to write again tomorrow and enclose you a receipt for some money which I shall express to you I hope dear you have rec'd the money which I sent ($100.00) some time ago. If not you will return the express receipt but I would advise you to make another application at the Express Office first as they may have discovered it you can call for the money and if you fail it may be best to send the receipt to me by Express. I have nothing to write this time Miss Berta Newell sends her regards & says you must write to her. we have dress parade every evening with Capt. Hanleiters Company,[3] We meet on half way ground- Crutchfield says our companies are getting very intimate. Write & let me know what you will do with Mary. Strawbridge will probably be down in 8 or 10 days. Love to all Your Affectionate Husband M.B. Ely

Did you get that money from Sam & Maje

---

[3] Captain Cornelius Hanleiter was born in Savannah in 1815. Although he opposed secession, with the coming of the Civil War, he served as lieutenant in several Georgia units. His primary duties involved constructing defensive installations around the city of Savannah. At the end of the war he had risen to the rank of Colonel (see People and Places). Henderson, *Roster of the Confederate Soldiers,* 4:240.

Sunday night, January 25, 1864

My Precious Love

Your missive of love dated 2nd inst was received yesterday evening pleased with no ordinary emotions of delight. darling you have no idea what a treat – your sweet sweet letters filled with affection are to me. You have no idea how anxiously I look forward to mail day and ______________________ if the little message of love should not arrive. Well darling I believe we have settled the questions about Mary's going to Savannah. Mr. Strawbridge is to leave next Thursday for camp I will send Mary by him and glad of the opportunity for I know that you and Dr. H are out of all patience. I have no news _____ only I hear that Mrs. Rutledge is to be married to Col. A. Redding[4] next week. I hope she will be satisfied after awhile, as it's her fifth husband. I have not yet taken my money out of the Express Office will send down for it tomorrow. Pa's cold is some better I think though he is suffering very much yet from his cough. The children all send love to you. Bessie says write her love right now. I told Eddie I was going to write you that he had been a bad boy, he begged me with great tears in his eyes to not write about him. I wish you could see him, he goes through wet and dry, hot and cold, he is perfectly taken with hunting rabbits – he goes every chance then you may look out for torn trousers and wet feet for he goes through mud and water and briers; he comes home a perfect fright with his pants slitted above his knees and the tatters a flying, like ____________ __________ in the wind. I can scarcely repress laughter I may be ever so vexed with the little "Rustic" Well love, I am not keeping house yet more than likely to be very soon. I have not __________ in buying any pork yet – and I fear it will be a grand failure, however I am obliged to keep Leasie awhile to spin her some clothes. I guess Pa will send a box to the boys before a

[4] Colonel A. Redding (Anderson Westmoreland Redding) married Mrs. Jane Rutledge in Harris County on January 26, 1864. They lived in the Ellerslie Community. Barfield, *History of Harris County,* 386.

great while I will then try to send you some butter. He may conclude to send it on with Strawbridge. Ma is writing to C.R.R.[5] and I guess she has detailed all the family news of importance. I write so often that I become perfectly threadbare for something to pen down. We are having some delightful weather here just now the hovering clouds broke in nearly a week since and it has been fair with not a cloud to mar the beautiful blue sky. I have not yet heard whether Mr. Garner has returned from Fla. have heard nothing from him since he left. I wish you would write to some friends about James ________ and try to get some syrup, some of the real genuine; if I only had syrup, I would not want much pork if you should succeed in getting the cases you can direct them to bring it up to Columbus in __________ with the wagon. I expect Mr. Green or Col. Redding would sell you some syrup. I do not like that made of millet[6]– however, I had rather have that than none I expect Uncle Billy McLeroy and Uncle Dick Thornton both have syrup to spair– but then it is so far to ship it – I expected to have written to Singleton for a supply but I learn through Mr. Swift's letter – he is in the war. I have written a long letter and you must pay back in the same coin. Good night, God bless and protect you my love, may all, write often to your wife, MFEly

Savannah, January 26, 1864

My Precious Wife

Your dear letter & the note in Sisters reached me by the same mail. I was delighted of course to get such an amount of reading matter. My love you seem to think I do not write to you often. I write every other day & I'm satisfied you ought to get a letter from me every mail. If you are not then there is most certainly something wrong somewhere that I can

---

5 "C.R.R." is a reference to Charles R. Russell.

6 Millet, or sugar millet, is a plant grown to produce sorghum for syrup. Guralnik, *New World Dictionary,* 902

not account for. I am writing this letter in Savannah I send today by express $150.00 and enclose receipt to you. I hope you will have no difficulty in getting this money. The agent at Savannah had __________ of Mr. Osborn instead of Mr. Osborn Ely. He says he will write to Columbus & direct the agent to deliver the package on to Pa if he will present the receipt. If it is not there, send me the receipt back immediately. I will send you $100 in a week or two. The pen will not write a word.

Your affectionate & devoted Husband MBEly

Tell Lizzy to learn to write so she can write Pa a letter tell Eddy to be a good boy & learn to spell and Pa will send him and Daughter something by someone passing. I would write more if I had a good pen MBE

Beaulieu, January 30, 1864

My Darling Wife,

I was just about replying to your precious letter received yesterday in order to send by mail but learning that Corpl Hubbard who has a furlough will go by Cataula I send by him hoping you will get the note a day or two sooner. My love I thank you a thousand times for your punctuality & for your sweet precious letters full of affection- Oh how I do appreciate those dear letters. They are ever doubly welcomed. I am glad you have at last disposed of Mary. I shall expect her tomorrow & then I hope she will be the bearer of a dear love missive from you darling. I write you so often I am afraid that my letters are not interesting particularly as I never have anything to write even of ordinary interest. you know a soldier's life in camp is one continuous round of monotonous duty without change or variation. I can only reiterate the same in substance every time I write – to wit that there is no news of importance that I can as well as usual & c. But ah! how thankful I should be for health when so many thousands of poor soldiers are prostrate on beds of sickness. Yes, I am thankful for health & more so is knowing that you & the children are well and doing well so long as I am assured of this I can be tolerably well contented. I received a letter from Sallie Dumas. She is a remarkably sweet girl & then she seems to love you so much that I have retaliated by taking a great fancy to her. She has received your letter & written again so I presume she has given you all the family news & I have formed the bad habit of writing very fast. If you have any difficulty in reading my letter let me know & I will be more particular. You know I can write a good hand when I exercise patience. Tell Eddy he must catch Pa a rabbit & that sister must learn to write & knit so she can write to Pa & also knit him a pair of socks. Remember to Pa & Ma and all the children. I hope Pa's cold is better, tell him to be particular and not expose himself. I shall send you a present soon either by Mrs. Railey or by express. I shall not tell you what I shall send.

Your very loving husband, MBE

Kiss the children for me if their faces are clean

Beaulieu, January 31, 1864

My darling wife

I received your very dear and affectionate letter from Mr. Strawbridge who reached camp today bringing Mary with him. It makes me very "proud" to receive letters from you so frequently. I think you do remarkably well considering you have but three mail a week & frequently have no opportunity of sending letters to the post office. I write almost every day for I am determined you shall not get ahead of me. darling you had stated that you received the money sent you express but you did not state whether it was the $100.00 or the $50.00 I sent a few days ago Please inform me as I am desirous that you should get all I send you. I am satisfied your palmetto is spoilt. I will dry the next lot I send You are mistaken about Dr. Brewster in other words you were misinformed. He has received no commission to raise a company. Palmer wrote a mistake about him hiring Mary. I simply told him he could have help as she was not hired at the Hospital. You wrote of provisions being high & scarce &c The Government provisions are doubled in price almost every month. We are now paying $2.10 per pound for bacon & everything else in proportion. If our pay is not raised we will starve to death (I mean the Officers) before the year is ended. You spoke darling of wanting to buy syrup from someone near Jonesboro. you can probably attend to that letter rather than myself. But I am fearful you will not succeed. I was shocked to hear of Uncle Billy's death. I loved him & I mourn for him as well as sympathize for his bereaved family. I shall write to Aunt Susan in a few days. I was truly glad to hear that cousin Ret's health was improving. I have thought of her many times lately & almost feared to hear from her direct lest I should receive the sad intelligence of her death. Darling are you compelled to use my old envelopes? I shall send you a lot of pens – ink- paper- envelopes – stamps &c when I send that present I spoke of in a previous letter The boys received their box, I did not ascertain what it contained. I am sorry my poor boy is sick – hope he is well by this time. Tell him Pa has two knives & will give him one – also will give Sister something nice Yours MBE

Savannah, February 1, 1864

My Darling

I resume my letter this morning in Savannah. I have a bad pen & must on that account be brief. I send you today by express a small box containing a few items which I trust darling will reach you in safety, I desire love to send you many needful articles & will do so if I can make arise. You are needing shoes I will try to send you a pair next month. It is still rumored that we go to the regiment in a very short time. I think we will go yet there are many who believe otherwise. Darling I have nothing more to write. My love to all If you are reading any letter you can not get in Columbus let me know and I will send it. The freight is paid on your box. Write often to your affectionate devoted husband MBE

Camp near Beaulieu, February 3, 1864

My Dearest Love,

I received your very welcome letter the 31st this evening. I was as usual very happy of the privilege of hearing from you. In fact I have no cause to complain of you – or the mails or any thing else connected with our correspondence, as I receive all your letters regularly. I wrote you yesterday enclosing a receipt for a box I have sent you which you will find in the Express Office (paid) directed to Mr. O. Ely. I merely call your attention to this for fear you may not receive the letter I wrote on yesterday. I should have stated in the outset that I send this letter by Mrs. Stott who will have it at Cataula in order that you may get it on Saturday. I will write again on Saturday that you may get it on Tuesday following. I am glad love you rec'd your Palmetto in good order. I was fearful it would spoil. Did Pa get his pipe & tobacco? The weather is clear but quite cool. I was down the river on Picket last night & an awful time I had. The wind sprang up about midnight & blew a perfect gale. The boat was tossed about like an egg shell & we could barely sit in it without holding on to something. The wind was so strong & the river so rough that we did not get to the battery until after eight o'clock. I am disposed to think however that our river Picket is almost played out. as it is now almost rumored to a certainty that we will rejoin the regiment at Red Bluff, S.C. in a very short time. I know we will miss our comfortable cabins at Beaulieu but we must make the change without grumbling, as it is the duty of all good & true soldiers. My dear you asked me if I did not short myself. I have plenty (such as it is) to eat and am otherwise comfortable & why should I spend what little cash I have – I wish I could send you ten times as much. A bill was passed in the low house of Congress allowing Commissioned Officers to draw rations of the same quantity and quality as the men & to purchase clothing of the regiment at cost. If this should become a law, we will have a little better showing than usual. I shall try to send you some more money – just as soon as possible. I suppose your school is in full blast ere this time. I hope you will not confine yourself too closely. My love to all – why do they not write occasionally? I do not hear from any of the family. Write dearest 3 times a week. Goodby Darling Your affectionate Husband MBE

Kiss the children. Tell Sister to read the new books Pa sent her – Will send Eddy a knife

Beaulieu, February 6, 1864

My Darling Wife,

I received your very dear and loving letter of 2nd inst last night. I can not thank you too much or too often for your kindness in writing so often to me. But for my life I can see why you would appreciate my letters so much as I never have anything worth writing. I imagine I am a very dull correspondent. In fact if there is anything I excel in I am well satisfied that it is not letter writing, for I have never had a talent for that sort of thing- I suppose I am writing my last letter from Beaulieu. we are loading our wagons and the command "fall in" will be given in a short time. As I have intimated in a previous letter, our destination is Red Bluff, South Carolina. We will be nearer Savannah than we are at present. Farewell Beaulieu! We go cheerfully – yet we know we are leaving all our comforts behind. Yesterday evening Capt. Hanlieter had an order published on dress parade complimenting the men of our command very highly. He thanked them for the manliness and cheerfulness with which they performed their respective duties. Also spoke of the humanity and cordiality that existed between the officers and men – saying – "We part with sorrowing hearts as Brothers" After parade we pressed the old Captain's hand in silence – as large tears trickled down his cheeks. It was an affecting scene. I will when the opportunity presents itself send you a copy of the order. Darling, I hope you have received your little box. I send you writing material I want you to use the ink I send you as your ink is so pail I have much difficulty in reading your letters. I am sorry I did not get your letter before I sent off the box so that I could have purchased such things as you desired. I can get you a nice gingham dress for 60 dollars. If you want it let me know, you need not trouble your self darling about sending butter or anything else. I am getting on very well and am not shorting myself. Tell Eddy and Lizzie to be good children and learn fast My love to Pa and Sister as well as all the rest I write next from Red Bluff goodby darling and believe me ever yours MBE

I write in great haste excuse it

Hardeeville, South Carolina, February 10, 1864

My Precious Wife

I wrote you a few lines when I first reached this place and as that letter was brief and unsatisfactory I will write again with more into particulars. We left Beaulieu on Saturday evening and reached Savannah with the Rose Dew troops next morning We took a steamboat down to Screven's Ferry on the Savannah River then we marched up the turnpike to Hardeeville at Col. Way's Head Quarters. The other companies went onto Red Bluff. Three companies of the regiment are camped about three one mile above us on the Hardeeville road The other companies are at Red Bluff. We are camped on a rice plantation and quartered in a rice mill. We have plenty of room in the mill & the houses around it. We have plenty to eat but nothing to cook it in as all our bedding cooking utensils &c are behind we expect them tomorrow. My repast has been quite thin of late I occasionally get a roasted potatoe – Sometimes, a slice of pork broiled on the coals and some real bonafide corn hoe cake based on a rusty weeding hoe. As to the sleeping arrangement they are only moderate. However there is nothing to do at night but to go to bed on a pile of rice straw, close your eyes and if sleep will come – what is the difference (As you are doubtless aware by this time you perceive that we are getting a little touch of the soldier's life A large battery is being built in a few hundred yards of our camp commanding New River bridge over New River This stream is near our camp and had to be choked with fine fish. I will test it soon. I can not as yet decide how I am pleased with the change – of course missing the comforts I left behind. The Company is generally well pleased. They can buy provisions in S.C. much cheaper than at Savannah. Besides they draw more rations &share the duty. I thought when I left Beaulieu I could soon get a furlough but Col Way says I can not get one for the reason that I have had one in the last six months. There will be no chance for me to get off before summer. I want you to come to see me in March. I can get you a nice house to live in and you can come direct to Hardeeville by Railroad. Let me know when you write again my love if you can come. I am holding this sheet of paper in my hand & writing on my knee – have not even a piece of plank hence you can account for the poor letter. I hope to get a letter from you this evening as I heard that Mrs. Brewster would be down to Savannah yesterday. My love to all. I am ashamed of this letter but have no way of doing better.

Your affectionate Husband, MBE

Hardeeville, South Carolina, February 15, 1864

My Precious Wife,

The last letter I received from you was dated the 2nd or 3rd of Feb. I understand from one of our men who went back to Beaulieu on business that Mrs. Brewster mailed a letter for me about ten days ago in Columbus, but I have never received it. I mailed a letter to you on the first day we reached this place sent one by Dick Russell a few days afterward, also one by Sergt Teel on day before yesterday. I suppose you have received some of these letters informing you of our changing camps from Beaulieu to Hardeeville, S.C. I have nothing to write that could possibly interest you. In fact I am completely at a loss what to say or rather what it suits in order to sill my sheet. Brother James is still at Beaulieu I can not imagine what has detained him there nor has Capt. Russell joined the company. I have received an order notifying me that he has been acquitted & ordering him to take command but he is still at Beaulieu. Bedell has a cold and is on the sick list and of course all the duty falls on me. I would rather have the itch than be in command of the company. It is a continual annoyance but no one can imagine unless he has experienced it. We have some sickness in our company now, principally colds probably contracted while on the march. I want to go to Savannah but it seems that I can not get off. It seems us officers must be the one left. There is something for me in the Express Office but I have not had the opportunity of getting it. I should be very pleased to see Cousin Ret. I hope her health will improve. Have you received your box? I was making some money while at Beaulieu. But I am not making any now. I shall try to send you some & forward at the end of each month. In my last letter I stated that there would be no chance for me to get home. According to an ordinance I will not be entitled to a furlough through the summer and by that time furloughs will be stopped. I want you to come down & spend a few weeks with me next month provided we stay here. Let me know my love what you will do. I am very thick headed this morning. You must look over a dull letter. I hope you will write often for I am very anxious to hear from you. I will look for a letter today. My love to all. Tell Eddy & Lizzy not to forget Pa. Goodbye darling, love

Your Affectionate Husband MBE

Savannah, February 17, 1864

My Precious Wife,

I received a letter from you today – a dear sweet precious dear-letter & of course I was delighted beyond all comprehension said letter was dated 12th inst I obtained 56 hours leave to come to Savannah on business. I was delighted to learn that you were well pleased with your dress. I am no judge of dress goods but I think I know your taste. I am very glad that the dress suits you my sweet darling for I love you so much. My love, I am always glad, yes happy when you are pleased. Capt. Russell has been acquitted. Tell Buddy I have got a pocket book for him full of little moneys. Sister is welcomed to her books – Give Cousin Ret my love. I could spin a few yarns that would please her were I at home. Goodbye my love - This is all the paper I have.

Adieu my loving wife ME

Hardeeville, South Carolina, February 20, 1864

My dearest Love,

We have been on South Carolina soil for two weeks and I have received but two letters from you, both of which directed to Savannah. Mrs. Brewster said she mailed one in Columbus but I never received it. I have mailed about half dozen letters at Hardeeville & I am afraid you have not received any of them as I have received no letters from you directed to this office. I hope though my love that our correspondence which has been somewhat deranged by my change will be more regular in the future. I was in Savannah on day before yesterday – received your dear letter which was a real treat it was __ good even till now to think about it. I write a short note in reply promising to write again at the camp. I am now trying darling to fulfill that promise. Sitting near my campfire, my paper before me on a board & that board on my knees I am trying to pen a short note to my distant loved one, my true and faithful, loving wife. I wrote to Pa yesterday. He may not get his letter before you get yours. Capt. Russell has been acquitted – Sgt. Land[7] has been elected 2nd Lieut Co H, 54th beating Dr. Brewster by about 10 votes. I believe that is all the news I have. Walter Brannon will come home in a week or ten days. I will send you some spool thread, if you want it. I should suppose it would cost more that if I would do, to express it. My love when I came to camp I tried to get the clothing we were speaking about, but they had received one order prohibiting selling to officers- hence I have but one pair of pants. my black ones have failed & my uniforms are nearly threadbare. I am almost barefooted my shoes having ripped from stem to stern. I will try to have them stitched. The weather is terribly cold. The north wind is fierce and not a tree or a bush to break it off. We will leave our quarters in the rice mill – will move out at the edge of the woods & occupy our tents & huts. I have two little pocket books, one for

---

[7] Aaron Land was a resident of Harris County and a member of the Russell Guards (see Co. H 54th "The Russell Guards" Biographies). "Mr. Aaron Land Dies Suddenly," *Columbus* (GA) *Daily Enquirer*, 12 October 1901, 5.

sister & one for buddy. I will send them by Walter Brannon[8] & send them some money. Dear you must write to me often – remember your letters are all the consolation I have. Goodby precious – Yours MBE

Hardeeville, South Carolina, February 23, 1864

My Darling Wife,

I had the inexpressible satisfaction of receiving two letters from you today – the first I have received from the Hardeeville Post Office. I was afraid some of my numerous epistles had failed to find their way to Cataula as I had been at this camp over two weeks & received no letters at this office. but, my apprehensions were happily quieted by the appearance of two dear loving letters today which were received with much real satisfaction and delight as well as sorrow to learn that so many of our ~~lettlives~~ relatives and friends have died. I was very much surprised as well as grieved of Uncle Blak Birdsong's death. I am sorry for Cousin Ret, I hope you will hear that her health is improving when she writes. My darling you sympathize with me for my rice straw bed for which I am much obliged. But after all, I fared pretty well taking everything into consideration. But I am "fixed" up now like a King. we have moved out by the road in the edge of the woods, as intimated in a previous letter I have my tent pitched and a brick chimney to it – the snuggest coziest place – you can't imagine! It matters not how cold the weather is – when I have my curtain closed and a good fire burning I can shed my coat and be perfectly comfortable Besides we have but little duty to perform. no river Pickets here – no Officer of the Day – and no Hanleiter. I have nothing to do but to write occasionally – Go fishing whenever I please and by the way there are more fish at this place than any place I ever saw

[8] Walter Brannon was a neighbor of the Ely family. He enlisted as a private in the Russell Guards on May 12, 1862. He was captured in Marietta, Georgia on June 18, 1864. He died in captivity at Martinsburg, Virginia (see Co. H 54th "The Russell Guards" Biographies). Henderson, *Roster of the Confederate Soldiers*, 5:701.

Perch – rock fish – Black fish – cats and trout besides other kinds We had a fine mess yesterday ("Rock and Jack") the nicest you ever tasted much better than the Beaulieu fish – as I was walking out on yesterday (Sunday) I met Sergt Hart and his wife with their fishing rods winding their way to the river. Then and there I drew a conclusion to wit – that it was disgraceful to see a man on the river fishing on Sunday. But to see a woman was ~~disgrace~~ disgusting! we heard this evening there had been a fight in Florida. The Yankees were falling back at last account. The 63rd Regt the one to which Rollen Russell was attached was cut up pretty bad – The Colonel was killed – the Lt. Col & Maj wounded Gen Beauregard is still sending troops there. A Regiment of Calvary in our immediate neighborhood left today. I hardly think we will go, yet I should like first rate to make the try [rest of letter missing]

Haven't time to look over letter to correct mistakes

Hardeeville, South Carolina, February 25, 1864

My Precious Wife,

Yours of the 22nd was received from George Stribling yesterday and was not expecting a letter through that source – it was indeed a surprise it seems darling that your letters were a little slow finding the new Post Office – but after the ice was broken they came in a perfect shower. On day before yesterday I received two letters – and I received them both at the same time both at once – writing a long letter. Lt. Bedell came in to my tent and handed me the third letter all in one day. I believe the last one of older date than others – yet for that reason I did not slight it Oh! no – on the contrary gave it an attentive perusal. Now darling as I have two more letters to answer I must try to spin out a long reply- but as I am already about to run aground I am fearful I shall not be able to write a very long letter – yet the longer it is the more tiresome it will be. Capt Russell is once more with the Company. He says that he will not accept a ten days furlough if he can not get longer. I shall try to get his ten days if he will not accept this. But I am afraid when he sees there is no chance to get longer than ten days he will gladly accept them. I dine on catfish pie for yesterday – we had plenty to spare – one of the blue cat weighted 9 lbs. we have plenty of fish then there are plenty of ducks, fish, turkey Deer – Bear &c in the river & swamp. Do you want a bear skin to make you a hearth rug? If so let me know. I will shoulder a gun and away to the river swamp. I will kill one & seek Bruins private retreat. By the way darling, you seem indifferent as to visit me this spring on account of a press of business &c. I shall be compelled to have you arrested and brought down. You will be compelled to succumb to military authority hence when I send for you report immediately to Hdqtrs & thereby escape being arraigned before a military tribune. By the way, what is Lizzie doing? If you have no use for her send her to me. She can make 30 (dollars a month __) for the Officers. Today is the 25th – the day you promised to write to me. It may as I am penning this note to you - that you are similarly employed - I shall therefore expect a letter in two days.

[Rest of letter missing]

Hardeeville, South Carolina, February 27, 1864

My precious wife,

I have an opportunity of sending you a note by Mrs. Hart, I write to you so often darling that you are apprised of almost every breath I take. Tomorrow, I shall go to Perrysburg picket taking with me nearly half the company. Perrysburg is a station on the railroad between Hardeeville and Savannah. I will have a good house to stay in & being on the Railroad I will get the news every day. I will have no duty to perform except to mount the Picket every morning and make the detail every evening. I suppose I shall have a good time especially if I get a letter from you every day. We will be stationed 3 miles from Hardeeville. I will dispatch my courier to the post office every morning. I shall also take pens, ink and paper so that I can write you several times during the week. I shall draw no more money till the new issue comes out as I suppose it will be better than the old. I have not heard from Dr. Houston since I left Beaulieu. I shall write him in a few days. I understand his wife is with him at this time .Some of our men who have been sick at Bethesda

Hospital came over a few days ago. they say Mary is very well satisfied. I will write Dr. H. to advise her to stay and do right. I write this in great haste as I am preparing to get off in the morning. We are messing with Jimmy, Jud, Sgt. McLeroy, Dowdell & Robinson. We have two negroes to cook for us. I have a good bill of fare generally. Jud and Robinson are going on picket with me as they are young & I am old and I will make them cook for me. Yesterday I mended my britches & I think it will make quite a creditable appearance. Somebody stole one of my hickory sheets. I think they will catch it if I can detect the party. This scattering letter must come to a close. Dear, you must not make sport of it, I wrote it in about three minutes.

Your Affectionate Husband, MBE

Perrysburg, South Carolina, March 1, 1864

My Precious Wife,

I wrote you a few lines by Mrs. Hart on yesterday just as I was about leaving for this place. This station is three miles west of Hardeeville and three miles from the Savannah River. The picket is kept at this point for the purpose of guarding the trestle work on the railroad. I am having a very good time, almost too good, as I have nothing to do but sit about the camp I get fatigued. I fish and hunt occasionally and fill out a portion of the time sleeping. The people in the neighborhood are very kind. They give us potatoes and such without any charge. If Sgt. Land passes the board I shall return to the camp next Monday & he will relieve me. Otherwise, I may stay here two weeks. I am perfectly satisfied to remain at this point as it is a higher pleasanter place than our present camp; besides the water is much better. The weather is quite warm and I am quite lazy – too lazy to write a legible hand. But you probably can read it darling –at least the greatest portion of it. & I guess at the balance. I suppose dear you have seen a list of the casualties in the late battle in Florida.[9] Capt. Mobley's company was terribly cut up. Kelon Watson was severely wounded in the knee- also Dr. Shannon's son was wounded in the knee, also another of the Watson boys was wounded. In fact a large number of his company were wounded & several (4 I believe) were killed. Darling, I have not received a letter from you in several days; in fact the last one was dated 22nd Feb. It is possible there may be a letter for me at camp. I shall go up to Hardeeville in the morning and mail the letter and perhaps get one from you, I hope soon. Love, I am afraid it will be many long months ere we meet again. I do not have any idea I can get another furlough as I shall not be entitled to one before summer and by that time furloughs will be stopped & in fact no one can form an adequate idea where we will be next summer – perhaps in Virginia or Tennessee. Therefore, as I cannot come to see you, can you come to see me? Yet we know in your __________ I do not like this endless separation love. I sit and think of you and my children continually from morning till night and then if I could see just a little probability of getting home to see you, I would be better contented. Your devoted husband, MBE Love to all, kiss the children, write soon lovely darling

Purrysburg Station, South Carolina, March 2, 1864

My Precious Wife,

Another day has been born away upon the wings of time & still no fond "billet doux" from my love. It occurred to me this morning that I would be rewarded with a short little message of love by calling at the Hardeeville post office. I accordingly went up this morning on the train__stalked into the Post Office but was doomed to disappointment.

---

[9] The Battle of Olustee was fought near Jacksonville, Florida in February 1864; it was the largest battle fought in Florida. Confederate forces drove the federal forces back to Jacksonville. The Confederate win prevented the Union from establishing control over northern Florida. "The Battle in Florida," *Macon Telegraph* (Macon, GA), 24 February 1864, 2.

By the way they have a very loose way of doing business at that office. I am afraid they are careless & let some of our mail get lost. But tomorrow may reward me with a letter. Oh! that it were tomorrow now. Today the weather is a bit cool but quite pleasant. Last night was warn of threatening rain. The fleas bit me all night. When I flinched on one side they would nab me on the other. Finally I had a dream in the midst of my trouble. I dreamed we were separated & that neither of us were the cause of it. It seemed that it became necessary for us to have our courtship & marriage over again. Consequently I commenced making love to my lady which was promptly reciprocated. Finally I proposed and was accepted (of course). I dreamed that I was very happy just at this crisis and sat down in a rocking chair taking you on my lap in order to set the day for our nuptials. Just at this time the fleas getting a little hungry renewed their attack and awoke me. After a spell I fell asleep & dreamed again. I imagined that I had caught a large flea and impaled him on the point of a pen knife. Col Way then requested me to hold up the flea in order that he might philosophize a little. Says Col Way if all the fleas in the world were properly dried their weight would be 400 tons __ and they could spin a web that would be as big as your leg and would reach out of sight. Now I have related my dreams love & you doubtless think I am getting very simple__ Expect you will send me a bag of marbles and a top by first passing if not sooner. Kiss the children for me I do want to hear from you my darling for I love you so dearly precious that I want to get news from you every day & hour. Goodby darling Good by sweet wife __ Your M.B.Ely

Camp Battery, Stephen Elliot, South Carolina, March 4, 1864

My Precious Wife,

Since date of last letter which contained my dreams I have been transferred from Purrysburg Station back to camp in my old quarters. I was not satisfied with the change but circumstances rendered it necessary. Lt Bedell has gone home on 15 day leave. Capt Russell has gone back to Beaulieu on 4 days leave. Sgt Land has not as yet gone before the board __ hence I was recalled to take command. The mail has just come in & still no letter. I cannot imagine what is the matter I have written six letters since I received one __ in fact I do not know what to think. I trust there is nothing the matter as surely I would have been notified. I have no news love, no not a single word. I will close this time. I will write again when I receive a letter from you.

Your devoted & affectionate Husband, MBEly

Camp Battery, Stephen Elliot, South Carolina, March 5, 1864

My Precious Wife,

At last I have been reassured and made to rejoice by the appearance of a dear and interesting letter from my devoted wife. It was dated 24th Feb. When I wrote last I notified you that I had returned to camp from the Picket Station on the Rail Road. Prior to my departure (which was sudden) I dispatched one of the pickets to camp on some business learning soon after myself I missed the Picket who had a letter for me. I remained at camp a day before I knew the letter had been sent to me. But, when I was informed that one of the men carried a letter for me I was determined to get possession of that letter as soon as possible. I sent a man after it to Purrysburg which is ten miles from camp & received it last night. I was very much relieved to learn that you and the children were in the enjoyment of your usual health. You spoke dear of sending some things by Walter Brannon. I cannot now say when he will be at home. But I can wait I suppose. I have patched & neatly mended my tattered garments and am now quite expert with the needle. I would have supplied myself with clothing at the Quartermaster's Dept. in Savannah, but previous to my application there had been an order prohibiting them from selling officers clothing. In fact, the Government has restricted the officers in clothing and rations & in fact everything. But, I suppose it is right as it gives the private a better chance. A private soldier in ranks is infinitely better off than a Lieutenant. But this is right. A private soldier should be the recipient of every favor the government can possibly bestow. If you should express my things to me perhaps it would be best darling to ship it to Savannah as we have communication with that town almost every day. Tell Sister & Buddy that Pa will send them their little pocketbooks as soon as possible. Say to Pa to drop me a line as soon as convenient. The boys are grumbling very much about not hearing from home. Judson is at Purrysburg. Bro. James is well and lively as ever. And Fannie Thornton is married we'll let her go it while young With all due respect to my darling and beloved wife__ I don't care if all the family marry

Your Devoted Husband, Marcus B Ely

I expect a letter this evening. I am satisfied there are several on the way. I have written about ten since you received the one you answered______________________ What becomes of them

Perrysburg, Picket Station, South Carolina, March 9, 1864

My Precious Wife,

After a short stay at camp I again find myself at Perrysburg Station, my old quarters of last week. I am under obligation to you darling for a sweet letter dated 3rd March which was received yesterday. I cannot describe to you the pleasure and happiness it affords me to receive letters from you. Neither can I picture the chagrin and disappointment I experience and it fails to come. Darling I write to you by Mrs. Hart & have wrote about five or six letters since. I do not believe you get more than half my letters. I write every alternate day & very frequently every day. But then if some of them get lost it matters not as I never write anything of much interest. I write often because I get lonely & writing you is employment to my mind & then I expect to hear from you oftener when I write often. Dear you may wish to know something about Perrysburg. It is an old Dutch town built around 160 years ago or about 70 years before the Revolution. It can hardly be called a town but rather the ruins of one as nearly all the houses have gone to decay. There is an old grave yard with dates as far back as 1751 on the tombstones. There is also the ruins of an old Dutch church – said to be the oldest church in the state. Besides many other curious things it is said the people lived on sturgeon stake and mulberry lace in the summer. They were very insolent & would fight in a minute. But, when the chills and fever pulled them down in the fall of the year they were very humble & submissive. My paper is nearly filled my pen is poor & I am out of ink. Good by Darling, I have dreamed of you 4 nights in succession.

Yours MBE

Perrysburg, South Carolina, March 11, 1864

My Precious Darling Love,

I have just been informed that Walter Brannon & Nathan McLeroy have furlough & will pass this place on the train this evening. I shall not have time to write a very long letter as the train will be on soon. I haven't much to write. I am sorry I am not at camp then I could send the children's pocket books to them. Besides, I could send home my flannel & overcoat. My darling you can send those things back by one of the boys – also have my hat fixed & send it back as I am needing it very much indeed. I went out driving for deer yesterday I took my stand at the edge of a swamp & waited patiently. Very soon the dogs started one & she saw me and stopped short. I took deliberate aim and missed her as clear as a whistle. The gun was at fault and not your humble servant. I write to you not a little darling, will be trying to get off in a few weeks but suppose I will fail. I am doing very well at this place. I go out with Dr. Hayes (a very clever man who was left at this camp) every day riding in his buggy. We have just returned from up the river and around old Perrysburg where we have been taking observations. We found a dog, _______, & a blacksmith. Also saw two fellows making arrangements to fish for sturgeon.

Goodbye darling, the train is coming. Yours, MBE

Purrysburg, South Carolina, March 13, 1864

My Precious Wife,

On yesterday I sent you a hasty note and sent it by Nathan McLeroy _ hope he will not keep it a week as the Honorable Mrs. Hart did & by the way my dear Mrs H told a deliberate lie when she said that Capt Russell would not give Brannon a furlough because you had written to me that Mr. Brannon was improving. But remember darling Ad Hart is a Jones & therefore you must make allowances. You know the Indian told two truths & one lie & thought he was doing well. If a Jones tells one truth (through mistake) & swears to two lies you may then give them all due credit. The very fact that Walter is at home proves the thing clearly though not to the credit of Ad Hart_ therefore darling, give yourself no trouble about it. Well, well I have written nearly a page and not said one word about your sweet letter which was received yesterday one dated 6th & the other 7th inst. I was extremely fortunate to get two at once, wish I could have the same fortune every day. Darling, I had forgotten in my previous letters to state there are several cases of smallpox in the vicinity of Hardeeville. I have to be vaccinated again but I am not afraid of it as I do not think it dangerous. I am going deer hunting today but am afraid I will miss the deer as I did two or three days ago. Tell the children Pa sends kisses to them & will write them a little letter next time. Darling you can send my things by Nathan McLeroy. Please have a pair of fine sowed shoes made & I will send the money to pay for them. I am barefooted. Goodby my precious darling I write in great haste & have a miserable pen__

Your devoted husband, MBEly

Savannah, March 15, 1864

Darling Wife

You have not written a line to me yet except the note Mary left with yours which I received the last of the week. I wish to hear from you occasionally dear, You must not expect me to do all the writing for I will be sure to scold you if you do not write soon. I am getting on as usual – am not improving – In fact I was not so well off yesterday as I was so prostrate that I was obliged to keep my bed all day. This morning I feel quite feeble but I am sitting up by the fire. Sister is in town. She has been to see me twice will come again before she goes back to Mr. Odoms. I hear Pa's Gin House was burnt down - I was very sorry to hear of his misfortune. I suppose our old buggy was consumed also – I went before the Board again on Monday but I have heard nothing from it. They promised to send up another application – but I suppose they intend to deceive me. I am looking everyday for my Uniontown furlough. love to Children & yourself darling Don't forget to write Your Devoted MBEly

Purrysburg, South Carolina, March 17, 1864

My Darling Wife,

Your precious little billet doux of 12th inst was received today & as I do not wish to remain long in your debt I will answer immediately. I was of course delighted to hear from you more particularly as your letter took me by surprise – or in other words came up on my blind side. I received it yesterday and answered it & now I am trying to scribble you another letter with my "gray goose quill" Darling I write you very often _______ In fact my letters are so frequent that I presume they represent every mail from Columbus to Cataula. It seems very natural though. But then as it is so natural for me to love you it should of course be perfectly natural to write often. It follows as a natural consequence. Love, I was very sorry to hear that Mr. Brannon's recovery was doubtful I am glad Walter is at home. You spoke dear of coming to see me in the summer. I hope to see you before that time darling. I cannot think we will be separated for two to three months longer without seeing each other. I hope something will turn up to my advantage. I am still at Purrysburg. I do not know when I will get back to camp I am very well satisfied at this place, have nothing to do from one day to another I have no company now. My friend Dr. Hazel[10] has left. I wish you were with me, I have a nice house & we could have a splendid time. I could make arrangements to stay at this place as long as I chose. Love, kiss the children for me. None of the family ever send one word to me. I will return their kindness by begging to be remembered by them once a month or oftener if they see proper, if not all right. The boys are well. Goodbye love may we meet soon is my paramount desire. Love, MBE

Savannah River Trestle, Perrysburg, South Carolina,
March 19, 1864

My Darling Wife,

I have nothing of interest to communicate – yet for the purpose of keeping up my old established habit of writing often. I will scribble a few lines. You perceive from the heading of my letter that I am still on Picket. I have not been to camp in two weeks will run down tomorrow to look around a little Will also go down on Tuesday as Nathan McLeroy will be due at Camp & I am expecting a letter &c. Lt. Bedell has returned from his furlough. Capt Russell I presume will be up next week. After his return I will put in a claim. I went up to Hardeeville this morning on the Train to see our Yankee prisoners captured on the South Carolina coast. Two of them were wounded after they were put on the train, a gold watch & all their over coats except those belonging to the wounded men was taken from them. I thought it looked a little niggardly – yet it was Gen Walker's order & had to be obeyed- If we should ever fall into their hands we may expect similar treatment. The ladies of Hardeeville I understand will have a Tableau in the rice mills which we formerly occupied near our camp. They failed to get a house large enough in the village. My love I hope I will get a letter today I am not satisfied if I do not get letters very often. My pen refuses to write & for

---

[10] Dr. Joseph Hazel was a physician in Beaufort, South Carolina (see People and Places). Dr. Joseph Hazel, "Find a Grave," last modified June 2015,http://www.findagrave/Dr. Joseph Hazel.

that reason I must close. Kiss the children for me I have nothing but a Goose quill to write with & it needs repairing & I have no knife. Goodbye Darling I must close God bless you my dear Your Very Loving Husband, MBEly

Battery, Stephen Elliot, South Carolina, March 22, 1864

My Precious Wife,

I attempt under very disagreeable circumstances to pen you a letter this morning. The weather is cold rainy & disagreeable in the extreme. The water & mud is all through my tent, but I have a bright cheerful fire blazing to compensate for all these inconveniences. You perceive from the heading of my letter that I have been relieved at the Savannah River Trestle. I came all the way to camp in the rain and found sheets of water and plenty of water in our flat encampment. As I am writing I learn that Nathan McLeroy is at Hardeeville waiting for a conveyance to camp. I am waiting impatiently as I hope he has a letter for me. I should have stated on the outset that I received your dear sweet loving letter on yesterday dated 14th inst. I love above all things to receive such tokens of love from you my precious wife – and to every song and every sentiment my fond heart will ever echo this truth - that the sweetest, purest treasure I have on earth is my precious wife. I also learn that Mr. Brannon is dead – also that Walter has not returned with the rest of the boys- I am very sorry for the family. Well dear I made a very considerable rise since I wrote last I have drawn from the government without money and without pride – one pair of pants – one coat- one pair of drawers – one shirt and one pair of cloth shoes – I shall send them all home. The old Governor Joe Brown supplied us with them. My dear I should have waited till Nathan came to camp before I answered your letter but I thought I would write again tomorrow. Nathan has just come but I have not time to read my precious letter that he has handed to me until I finish this as the man is waiting impatiently for this letter. Yours MBE I'll write again tomorrow.

Camp Battery, Stephen Elliot, South Carolina, March 24, 1864

My Precious Wife,

I received your dear letter by Nathan McLeroy just as I was in the act of finishing one to mail to you. Have since received one dated 18th inst of older date. I promise to write a reply to the one received by Nathan & I will now attempt to answer both of them. But I have been writing under sundry difficulties= to wit – a bad pen – bad paper & a tremendous cold morning. I suppose love you are experiencing this weather yourself & of course I can tell you nothing about it. Love you asked what kind of shoes I wanted, Please have made of calf – high quarter and sewed, I want them made substantial. I will forward the money to pay for them. When I go to Savannah again I will try to get you a nice pair of Garter boots for I know you need them. I also want to send you in the course of a month $100.00 of the new issue. You said something darling about my coming home as soon as possible on furlough. That is impossible my love I can not make an application before the first of summer & by that time in all probability furloughs will be stopped. Besides, it is now thought we will go to Virginia towards the latter part of Spring & our places will be supplied with old men and broken down regiments. The Yankees have threatened to march on Richmond with 250,000 men & Gen. Lee will have to be reinforced with a large army. Capt. Russell will be up soon. He has applied for 30 or 40 days furlough. He will be absent nearly all the spring. Darling you said you wanted to see me more than ever you did before. I can say the same my precious – But I honestly confess I do not think I will enjoy that happy – joyous glorious privilege in <u>many many</u> long days. I do not wish my precious to deceive you by stating that I will be at home soon for there is no possible chance for me to come. I thank you a thousand times darling for your kindness in sending me some things to wear I hope my hat will be sent as I need it sadly. I will send you all my new clothes & shoes &c and you can sell them. Also I will send Eddy some iron marbles to play with. You must explain to him that the Yankees shot them at us.

Also, I will send their pocket books & money. Kiss the children & excuse this awful scrawl Yours MBEly

Camp Battery, Stephen Elliot, South Carolina, March 25, 1864

My Precious Wife,

As I have supplied myself with a new pen and some good paper I can not refrain from writing you a short letter this evening. I have been nearly out of paper for several days and was often troubled to get it on order to write to you. But love I will have paper if it costs $20.00 a quire You intimated in one of your letters Darling that paper was getting scarce with you. When I return the trunk you will find pens ink paper envelopes &c provided Darling I have an opportunity to buy these things. I think I can get you large cap paper at Coosawatchie 30 miles from Hardeeville on the Savannah and Charleston Rail Road. I understand everything and especially stationery is much cheaper than at Savannah. I received a note from Dr. Houston today. He is well, but says the company stationed there is very noisy & disturbs him. You know he has moved up near his coast house. He did not mention Mary but I presume she is getting on well. Precious I have not a word of news. Nearly all the Calvary around us are under marching orders. They will be sent to Richmond. I suppose Uncle Jeff is anticipating another raid __ or perhaps as I anticipated in a previous letter __ he is looking out for another "on to Richmond" The morning paper spoke of "recognition" and "Peace Meetings" at the North __ in my opinion all Humbug. Precious since I wrote last we have had a considerable quantity of rain. But this morning the weather cleared and we have a beautiful spring air. I went down to the river to fish today __ but the tide was so high they (the fish) would not bite and becoming fatigued as well as disgusted I quit fishing and came back to camp thinking I could employ myself more agreeably by writing to my precious wife. When I left the Savannah River Trestle last week Jud remained up there with Lt. Bedell to make the details. He (Jud) is having a good time __ has nothing to do but cook his meals & ride up to and from Hardeeville on the train. Jimmy is well.

He has purchased a pig & he is very busy at times feeding & attending to him. When it rains he makes a pen for his pig in his kitchen. I told him he had better take the pig to bed with hm. I hope Darling you will send my hat if possible as my cap is worn out and I can not get another. Besides summer is coming on & I want something to shade my head from the sun. Darling what has become of your brother James Dumas people? When I was at Beaulieu I heard from them occasionally; but since we left not a word. I suppose they know where I am. Well Darling I am drawing to the end of my sheet Kiss the children for me & tell them to kiss Ma for Pa. Goodbye Darling love you MBE

Hardeeville, South Carolina, March 26, 1864

My precious Wife,

Your dear little note was perused today with infinite satisfaction Walter B having reached camp today. You spoke of mailing one the day before. It seems that Walter is the most expeditious mail carrier – as I have not received the letter referred to. I sent to Hardeeville today in order to ascertain if the trunk had arrived but heard nothing from it. In looking over the Express list in the Savannah paper of today I notice that there is freight for W.B. Ely I do not know anyone by that name – It may be my baggage, but I have no idea when I can ever have an opportunity _ my darling to go to Savannah. Capt Russell will probably leave in a day or two on Forty days furlough Lt Bedell is on picket & I will not be allowed to leave the camp on any pretext whatever, I am sorry the trunk was sent on by Walter Brannon or expressed to Hardeeville SC But it makes no particular difference as I will get it sometime. I hope love you will send my hat. I have nothing to wear on my head but an old tattered cap & I can get nothing better. Please send it to me as it is _ as I am compelled to have something on my head My cap is no protection besides it is worn out entirely. Please darling put it in a box and direct it to Hardeeville So. Co. I hope you will send it immediately if you possibly can. I have nothing new to write darling _We are all doing the best we can. I am quite well except a cold. Everytime there is rain I get my feet wet in this miserable muddy sloppy country which causes me to take cold. Darling I have written in great haste. You must look over a dull letter I wish you had some of the nice paper I am writing on. But I shall send you some large size so that I may get long letters from you. Yes, Yes darling as you say we are doomed to this separation _ but you know you can come to me if I can not go to you. Yours MBE Your ink was so bad _ I mean so pale _ I could not read all your letter Kiss the children & tell them to look at their little letter

Hardeeville, South Carolina, March 29, 1864

My Darling Precious Wife,

I have just returned from Savannah and am now at Hardeeville waiting for a conveyance to camp. I went down to Savannah on yesterday in order to look after that trunk. I found it all right & am now under a thousand obligations to you for your kindness darling I have not had an opportunity recently to write you a very long letter_ But then I never have much to write. Yesterday & today are the first days in some weeks that I have been at leisure – In fact I have either been on Picket or in command of the company nearly all the time I have been in SC. The duty however is remarkably light. The only objectional feature in this case is the confinement. Love I suppose I will receive a letter from you when I reach camp as some of the boys on Picket in this place said there was one in the office for me on yesterday. I wish I could get a letter from you everyday. It is such a rich treat darling to get your dear loving letters for then I know I read the sentiment of a true and loving heart. My faith in your true devotion darling is strong and abiding. But my faith in the love of others is not as large as a grain of mustard seed _ "Actions speak louder than words &c &c" I am somewhat indisposed today nothing serious though I had some fever last night – Several of the men have been complaining the same way – but it generally wears off in a few days. I will return the trunk in a few days with some things. Kiss the children Goodbye my sweet darling Yours MBE

Hardeeville, South Carolina, March 30, 1864

My darling,

As I have just written and dispatched a letter to you I will be brief this time. I merely wish to notify you my sweet wife that you will find the trunk at the Express Office Columbus GA whenever you call for it. I send the overcoat_ two jackets_two pr pants_two pr socks_ 2 shirts_ 3 or 4 pr Drawers, 1 pr cloth shoes 1 pr old boots _ some paper a few envelopes Eddie & Lizzie's pocket books Eddies grape canister shot for marbles 1 vest _ some beans for I know you love to eat them – love to string them & love to drink the soup & perhaps other things that I forget – But it is unnecessary to enumerate them as they will all be in the trunk when you get it. Darling you may dispose of those shoes jackets and new pants if you choose. Perhaps you can trade them to somebody for their negroes to wear and get some gray Janes in return to make me a nice jacket. I am very anxious to get a jacket. I have no chance now to go to Coosawatchie to buy stationery. The paper I send will last till I have an opportunity of sending more. Tell Eddie these iron marbles I send him are the kind the Yankees shot at us out of their cannons. As I am a little indisposed tonight you will please excuse a short dull letter darling __ Thank you again for your loving kindness for the eggs. I love you all the more everyday.

Kiss the little ones and may God bless you all ____ MBE

Hardeeville, South Carolina, April 2, 1864

My Darling Wife,

This is Saturday night. Of course I'm thinking of the loved ones at home. On Saturday nights my fond memories seem to go back more vividly than any other night. I can imagine us darling sitting around our cheerful fire – our little ones perchance have gone to roost. Our tubs of water are soon brought into requisition & then such splashing in the bath concluded and then a double enjoyment – a clean person & clean linen. But why pursue this further I trust Love the day of our reunion is not very far in the future. You know the war cannot last forever; if I should be so fortunate to see its conclusion. Darling, I have no news as usual. Last evening I was invited to Col. Way to coffee. We had a nice supper & I did it ample justice. I have an awful cold and cough. I shall bathe my feet tonight and tomorrow I will try to get some medicine for my cough. I must close darling as I have nothing of interest to write about. Kiss the children and write soon to

Your affectionate and devoted Husband, MBEly

P.S. [April 3] My darling the key was sent by mail You will find it at the Columbus PO I have a pair of woolen socks a pr of drawers & a vest I will send when the weather moderates. My cold is better this morning I send you a Receipt You will find it paid Capt R has 40 days furlough Suppose he will be up soon MBE

Savannah River Trestle, April 8, 1864

My Darling Wife,

I cheerfully begin the pleasant task of writing you a letter. It is always a pleasant duty but not half as pleasant to send to you as to receive a letter from you. I wrote on day before yesterday & sent it to the post office at Hardeeville. The messenger gave the letter to Henry Kennon[11] who was on his way home. He therefore instead of mailing it put it in his pocket to carry to you. So he informed me as he came by on the train which was all right. Therefore you received two letters from me - but as usual they are very dull and uninteresting. I am at the Savannah River Trestle and likely to remain here for some time. I am very well satisfied – have no one to trouble me _ being nine miles from the company. I can go to Hardeeville on the train whenever I please - stay as long as I please and come back on the train the same way. The conductor always stops at this place for the accommodation of myself and pickets. I frequently get on the train and go down to the Savannah river Bridge which is about

[11] Henry Kennon was a member of the Russell Guards (see Co. H 54th "The Russell Guards" Biographies). Henderson, *Roster of the Confederate Soldiers*, 5:705.

three miles from the foot of the trestle. The Trestle is a vast framework for the train to run on twenty feet high passing through a dismal swamp full of cypress trees and other growth to say nothing of Deer, Turkey, Bears, Squirrels, rackcoons, otters, Beavers, alligators and everything else. There are also thousands and tens of thousands of owls & such hooting among them you can't imagine. I get as many fat squirrels as I want to eat. I killed five yesterday. The River is now too high for fishing. In fact it is over five miles wide – having completely inundated the rice plantations and its lakes. A few days ago I borrowed a gun from a war widow that lives close by to kill a mess of squirrels. When I returned the gun in the evening I sent her a mess of squirrels and told the messenger to tell her that if she would let me borrow the gun again I would kill her a mess frequently when I was supplying myself. She sent the squirrels back stating that she never eat one in her life but I could borrow the gun whenever I want it. The people are very kind in S.C. but some of them are very curious they scarcely ever eat bread and never saw any lye hominy much less eat it. Your loving Husband Ely

Savannah River Trestle, April 13, 1864

My Darling Wife,

By the way, I have just learned that Ashfield[12] of our own company would pass down on the train this evening on his way home offering me an excellent opportunity to surprise you with a billet doux. I wrote you today and mailed it at Hardeeville hence you will get two letters bearing date 13th inst. I acknowledged three letters in my last which was mailed today. You will therefore get the two of the same date as was the case when Kennon went home. I am sorry when I write a despondent letter to you. I am sometimes guilty of that. You know there can not be sunshine all the time. Occasionally a lowering cloud will obscure the bright clouds of our existence – occasionally the sea of our life is rendered turbulent by

---

[12] Joseph Ashfield was a member of the Russell Guards (see Co. H 54th "The Russell Guards" Biographies). Ibid., 5:700.

the winds of adversity. But darling I have been in the army so long having stared reality in the face that I can not cut a very fantastic figure therefore I will drop metaphors and tell you of a beautiful dog hide one of my friends dressed and gave to me. I expect to have a pair of gauntlets made that will reach about to my elbows. I would not take $25.00 for the hide; it is a beautiful yellow color. Darling, what are eggs worth in Harris I pay $2.50 per dozen for all I buy. If you can get them for $1.00, $1.50, please send me a few by Ashfield. I would "relish" them as Brown would say. I am "sending up" some "red faces" for you, you know that is the name of the new confederate money. I have not drawn any money in some time or I could send you some by Ashfield. When Judson or Jimmy come I will send you some also some rice if I can get it. I told you in my last darling that the trunk key was sent by mail to Columbus directed to you. I suppose you have got it by this time. I hope son and daughter have their little picket boys & their money. tell Eddy he must come down and bring sister and we will go out & catch some fish. Darling I haven't a word of news. We are enjoying some beautiful spring weather hope it will last. My darling you must write a long letter by Ashfield when he comes back and give me all the news &c. The train is not far off & I must close – My love to all - Tell sister to send me a piece of wedding cake as long as old Beck mule's head or longer if convenient. Your loving MBE

Savannah River Trestle, April 16, 1864

My Darling Wife,

I have dispatched you such an amount of voluminous epistles recently thereby making such heavy demands on my limited stock of information – that I am about "broke." Hence love as I am a bankrupt correspondent you will at least excuse me this time if I "cut my garment according to the cloth" and for once give you a short note. Darling I acknowledge with many thanks your dear favor of 10th inst which was received on yesterday. I have rec'd four letters from you this week & I have had a rich heart I assure you. Dear I will have an opportunity of sending you a letter by Mrs. McLeroy who will be at home about the middle of next week. I learn that the Secretary of War has issued an order stopping all furloughs. I had been expecting it for some time. In fact I have long since given up all hope of seeing you and the darling children this year at least for I think we will go to Virginia in about six weeks – In fact there is a rumor afloat that we will be sent to North Georgia in a short time. But I have reason to doubt this report as I have learned they are sending troops from the Western Army to Virginia – where the great battle of the war will be fought this summer the great battle that will decide the destiny of our beloved country. Darling I have nothing to write in the way of news. I am plodding along on picket as usual. I have no idea how long I'll remain at this place – perhaps two or three weeks longer before I am relieved. Love to all & to the children I must close now as my paper is about out. Your Affectionate Husband MBEly

Savannah River Trestle, April 18, 1864

Darling Wife,

I have an opportunity of sending a note by Mrs. McLeroy also a small box which she says she will deliver to you. I have a few articles of clothing I do not need vig– a pair of woolen socks, two pair drawers, (I have three pair besides them) also my vest. I send you a little inferior paper and a few envelopes. I would send more but I am still on Picket & have no opportunity to get any money to purchase paper and envelopes. I suppose you need me to send you a good supply. I send you a few ____ ____ I have on plus shoe strings made of squirrel hide. Darling I have nothing that will interest you. If I could always make my letters interesting I would write everyday – but I will be sure to write often enough anyhow. The weather is cool and unpleasant and while I am writing it is raining very rapidly. Oh, Darling I want to see you worse than ever before. We have been separated for four long months and no prospect of seeing each other in another four months.

Your Devoted, MBE

Undated [possibly late April 1864]

Darling I will write you a tiresome lengthy letter this time if you manage to "wade" through it. Your patience is rare! The court martial is not sitting, hence I go back to Hardeeville tomorrow morning – to fix up my traps- then away ____ us to Dalton. I shall send my trunk home & a few things I can spare. I shall need very little. Well love about my shoes, they fit splendidly & I am very much Pleased (Had to make a capital "P") indeed with them. I shall have to split them a little to make them go on easy but that will not injure them at all. Darling, Dr. Houston will express 50 Dollars to you sometime during the month of May. I shall instruct him to do so before I leave. If you need any money before that time let me know Darling and it will come. I have been trying hard to get some money but I have so far failed. Capt. Clark, our QM could not make arrangements to get it, so we are compelled to go without it. Darling, I shall leave early on the train in the morning – or I would be glad to send the children something to keep up their expectations or rather I should say to satisfy their expectations. [Missing portion] ____ with the most intense fury and the missiles of death fly thick and fast, I shall not quail but stand as firmly as a rock, let the consequences be as they may. Darling, I have written you rather cool letters heretofore when I have met with a disappointment – But I do not desire to do so. Of course I can not but harp a little on my disappointment. You know darling, you and my children are my all – my precious jewels- for they are set in my heart. they are my throne around which is centered every hope – everything worth a thought in this life that appertain to this mundane sphere. Dear, I have written this long letter in the midst of a great "stir and bustle" An Italian is playing on the harp – some of the "Boys" are dancing & some of them drunk. Hence in the midst of this confusion my letter must partake of it. Love in conclusion I will say that I will write again once or twice before I leave. No news- except war excitements – Thousands of troops are going off on every train to Kingston & Dalton, GA. The two great strategic points – My love to Pa and Sister & all the family. Kiss the children & believe me Precious wife – ever thine. MBEly

Hardeeville, South Carolina, April 24, 1864

My Precious Wife,

I hasten to pen you a short note this morning. Our regiment has been ordered to Dalton, GA - We will leave just as soon our Col. Harrison's Regt relieves us which will be in two or three days. This move takes me by surprise as I believed we were going to Virginia. Thousands of troops are pouring by everyday "en route" for Virginia. The last letter received from you darling was dated 25th last. I have written more than a half dozen times since - I am extremely anxious to get a letter before we take up our line of march. There will be no mail today as it is Sunday & if I do not get one tomorrow I shall leave disappointed. Oh yes I remember Ashfield will come today. I expect to get a letter from him. ________ will be on tomorrow or next day. I shall be in Savannah Wednesday to attend a court martial as a witness – will not probably return to South Carolina. Direct reply to this Dalton, GA. Goodbye Darling Wife – that whatever fortune or misfortune is mine is nothing more than falls to lot of all –

Your Devoted Husband MBE

Dalton, May 2, 1864

My Dearest Darling,

We arrived at Dalton this morning 4 o'clock. We were put on open boxes at Atlanta & of course suffered some during the night as there was a light frost to be seen this morning. This is the dirtiest, nastiest place I ever saw – mud and filth everywhere –nothing to be seen but soldiers moving in every direction. It is said Gen. Johnson has about 100,000 men and will be sure to whip the enemy whenever the battle comes off. But, as I intimated yesterday- a great many think the Yanks will not fight unless forced to it - a large part of the Yankee Army go out of service in 8 days – that is the 10th of this month and it is thought that these fellows can not be brought to the ____________. Darling you must excuse me for writing on the back of an old letter. I have neither money-paper-envelopes-stamps-ink – nor in fact hardly a change of clothing having left nearly everything in Atlanta. Love I am quite anxious to get news from you and the children. I shall go to the post office directly – but I do not much expect a letter today. Darling, I have not had an opportunity of looking about & of course cannot tell you much about this country – But what I have seen of it – very hilly and mountainous. It is thought we will go in Walker's Division – We are in Mercer's Brigade. I do not know whether we will go to the extreme front or remain near Dalton. I shall know by the time I write again. The boys are well and in good spirits. I caught a fall this morning before day & bruised one of my legs –but I'm able to get on very well. Kiss the children. You will find my old trunk (express paid) at the Express Office Columbus Write often darling, I am always anxious to get letters from you. I shall write again soon. Love to all. Your devoted, MBEly

Dalton, May 3, 1864

Darling Wife,

We remained in Dalton until this morning when we left for our camp which is about four miles due east. We have struck a new camp in the woods and have a very pleasant place and good ____________ ___ __________________ Since besides we are all well and in excellent spirits. Now darling, I have told you about all that would interest you. I write a few lines this time, not that I have any news but more particularly I wish to enclose you an express receipt. I forgot to tell you in my previous letter I saw a large number of Yankee prisoners before I left.

The Russell Guards (Co. H, 54th Reg.) and the rest of the 54th Infantry arrived in Dalton on May 2, 1864 at the outset of Sherman's Atlanta Campaign. They joined Major General W. H. T. Walker's Division along with the 57th and 63rd. The infantries were under the command of General Joe Johnston. By May 7, they were actively involved in the Battle of Rocky Face Ridge, two miles northwest of Dalton and about 80 miles from Atlanta.

The North's target was the Western and Atlantic railroad, the supply line to Atlanta.[13]

Taylor's Ridge, May 9, 1864, 8 o'clock a.m.

My own Precious Wife,

Since date of last letter we have moved up on Taylor's Ridge and now in line of battle. The fight had partially opened on our left. There is very heavy skirmishing and the prospect for a battle imminent. Darling you must be content this time with a short note. I will write in more detail when I have leisure. Kiss the dear children. Goodbye my love. Bless you and the precious children. In haste darling, Your devoted Husband I dreamed of you last night.

Bivouac, near Calhoun, May 13, 1864

My Precious Wife,

Your precious letter dated May 8th and you may be very sure I was very delighted to get news of my darling wife. I am very thankful my sweet wife for your kind remembrances of sending money. But please you do not need to send any more. I have no use for money, only to buy stamps or whatever. Since I wrote that note stating that I had no paper, I have received more than I want and wish you had a portion of it. We are now one mile from Calhoun. Walkers & Loving's Divisions composing the left wing of Johnston's Army. Of course we are having a rough time but the boys are well & in good spirits – ready and able to whip the Yanks- or at best to do their full part. Darling, I will again remind you that I want neither money or clothes sent to me if I had in a clothing store. I could only carry what I have on my back. My mattress – bed

---

[13] Matthew J. Gallman, *The Civil War Chronicle, The Only Day-by-Day Portrait* (Old Saybrook CT: Ancourt Press, 2000) 411.

quilts are at Dalton, also all the clothing I have on. I carry my haversack[14] containing my paper, brush, Bible & rations – also my blanket and pillow on my back rolled up in a bundle – These together with my pipe, canteen and sword constitute my load on a march. We have had awful cold weather I should have suffered – had I not piled down with the boys. Darling, I have not given you much war news – You can see that in the papers – We are on the left and all the fighting is from fifteen to 30 miles from us. We can have the booming of the cannon & know that there is fighting going on every day – we all hear that the Yankees have assaulted could not bring them. Dear I have several quills & pens and envelopes. I am sure you are distressed about my clothing arrangement. It makes no kind of difference with me love that I have no clothing with me. A portion of my clothing are at Atlanta and the remaining at Dalton & we are now 30 miles from Dalton. We are near Calhoun, passed through Resaca last night. We are constantly marching, In fact we are called _______ with knapsacks and of course lastly I will try to get a letter pieced together[15]

Bivouac, Mercer's Brigade, May 15, 1864

Darling Precious Wife,

We are in a mile of Oostanaula River – 3 miles west of Calhoun at which pleases me. Have been since 9 o'clock this morning. We left our entrenchments at Resaca last night – marched all night. Our army is not falling back we are trying to head off the Yanks who are striving might & main to flank us. Gen. Walker's division is here. The enemy are entrenched above named river in one mile of our line of battle. We dared them for a fight today and was accommodated – Jackson's Brigade

---

[14] A haversack is a knapsack used for carrying personal articles. Varhola, *Life in Civil War America*, 251.

[15] On May 9, Johnston's army was facing Sherman's three divisions near Calhoun. It was at this point that Marcus felt his mortality. The words he penned in his Bible were very telling. On May 15, Sherman sent a division to cut off Johnston's supply lines and Johnston was forced to pull back. Boatner, *The Civil War Dictionary*, 691–92.

charged them into their breastworks. They were forced to pull back being heavily pressed by a very superior force. Our loss was considerable. They (the Yankees) do not seem anxious to fight. I learned our army has repulsed them all along the line which is now nearly 40 miles long. We are having a pretty hard time marching to & fro but we are getting accustomed to anything and all are in fine spirits. On yesterday we were drawn up in line of Battle at Resaca. We were under a heavy fire of grape & shrapnel, but we all escaped in our company except one man who received a slight wound in the arm. A lieutenant and several men in the right were badly wounded. Lt. Thomas, Co. G[16] was slightly wounded by a mini ball in the face. Two men were killed in the 63rd, A G. Our general says we will be sure to whip them. There are ten thousand rumors – in _______ which I will not pretend to give. Well darling, enough about war I am heartily tired of it. I have heard the booming of cannon and the rattling of small arms until it sounds monstrous. There has not been a moment of time during the day – when there was not fighting somewhere on the line. But I will drop the subject. I trust our little boy is not having a bad time with his measles. I have not written very often _____ darling – always writing in a great hurry but you will look over a hasty and disconnected letter. I will close Precious one. It is necessary to reiterate the love which ______ in my bosom. My precious loving wife and children. Love to all and especially you and the children. Love, MBE

Our loss at Resaca was considerable especially in the artillery. I saw many wounded.[17]

---

[16] Lieutenant Grisby E. Thomas enlisted in the 32nd Regiment, Co. G; he later transferred to Co. G, 54th Infantry. Henderson, *Roster of the Confederate Soldiers*, 6:781.

[17] Losses at Resaca were heavy on both sides. The Union losses were 2,747 and the Confederate losses were 2,800. The total for both sides was 5,547. "Resaca Battlefield," last modified 2014, http://www.civilwar.org/battlefields/resaca.html.

Saturday, May 16, 1864

May 7th was ordered to the front

8th went into line of battle at Rocky Face Ridge

9th ordered to Resaca which we reached at 3 o'clock

May 10th 11th marched a few miles South and returned to the same camp midnight & went on picket

12th took up line of March for Calhoun which we reached midnight

13th rested

13/14 ordered to Resaca where we were in line of battle in a galling fire for several hours – at midnight were ordered to Calhoun reached it at day break

15 – went into line of battle west of Calhoun[18]

Bivouac, near Kingston, May 18, 1864

My Darling Precious Wife,

Owing to our retrograde movement I have not written you in three or four days at least I have not mailed a letter. I wrote a few days ago but not having an opportunity of sending it I destroyed the letter. I was delighted darling to receive your last letter – glad to hear that our little boy was getting on well with the measles. Bro James also rec'd a letter from Sister – I am glad she is able to write. Well love, here we are below Kingston – 50 miles below Dalton. I shall not attempt to give the reason for this movement on the part of Gen. Johnson. I am satisfied he knows what he is about & besides you will hear before many weeks the complete overthrow of the Yankee Army. We have had a hard road to

[18] Between May 15 and May 18, the Confederate soldiers marched to Resaca, back to Calhoun, and then to Dalton and Adairsville with skirmishes along the way. The Confederates moved into Adairsville, hoping to find a valley wide enough to effectively face the Union forces. Johnston was unable to find a suitable valley to place his troops, so they withdrew. Geoffrey C. Ward, *The Civil War: An Illustrated History* (New York NY: Alfred A. Knoph, 1990) 320–23.

travel for some days past. The Enemy has pressed us very hard and we were under a forced march all the time. We fought there all the evening yesterday at Adairsville & left at Midnight & reached this place this afternoon. The men are completely "ragged out." Jimmy and Jud stood the march first rate and so did I. We are all well. I never felt better in my life except that I am somewhat fatigued and foot sore. In the series of engagements from Dalton to Adairsville we have invariably whipped them back & of course their loss is heavy – ours comparatively light. We have a good many wounded in our army. You can get the news from the papers – therefore I will not attempt to give anymore. Of course the people at home will think we are ruined- but they must wait patiently the issue. We will move again tonight- I think we will make our final stand – below the Etowah river which is 8 or 10 miles below. Darling, you must excuse me this time I wish to rest before we march again. My love to all at home – also to our children – Goodby this time my precious darling wife Write to your MBEly

P.S. I have received all the letters you have written me Tell Ma I have not heard from George since he was sent to the hospital. Albert McCants[19] from company is missing – has not been seen since the two days fight at Resaca Suppose he is a prisoner MBE

Bivouac, near Etowah River, May 20, 1864

My Precious Wife,

I wrote you a few days ago – but am not certain the latter was mailed. After I wrote this letter our brigade was ordered back to bring up the rear- The Yankees were pressing us very hard and I gave the letter to a teamster to mail. We are now on the north bank of the Etowah River. I suppose we will cross over to the south side this evening. On yesterday

---

[19] Albert McCants was captured at Resaca on May 16, 1864. He died of typhoid fever in a military prison on May 31, 1864 (see Co. H 54th "The Russell Guards" Biographies). Henderson, *Roster of the Confederate Soldiers*, vol 5:705.

we fully expected the big fight would open. Our army was drawn up in line 3 columns deep extending many miles east and west – our center resting in a wide valley and the right &left wings extending across the hills. The day before we skirmished with them all day and of course we expected to fight them today- But, during the night they moved rapidly to our left and tried to flank us – we fell back to this place leaving our chosen battle ground 3 o'clock in the morning. We are fatigued but enjoying good health. Bro. James is back with the wagons. He is not very well & we sent him with the wagons to recruit and rest. He has stood the long fatiguing marches much better than anyone would suppose. I assisted him along by carrying his musket occasionally. Jud is well but the heavy marches have made his jaws look rather sharp. I have not heard a word from George, if you have heard from him let me know. We are receiving reinforcements daily. When we get a chance at the Yankees, we'll make a telling blow. I will only write what concerns our regiment. On yesterday we were in a line of battle in an old field on a high hill, above us the enemy planted a battery & commenced shelling us. Many shells passed over us & some threw dust and dirt on us. It made us feel a little spotted as they had all the advantage – but none of our regiment were injured, expect heavy fighting. Darling it would be worth a thousand dollars a minute to be with you and the children now but that is like the "negroe's possom" -too good to talk about. I hope there is a better day coming. Oh! Were it not for that hope I would die of despair. Every minute you are in my thoughts – in my heart – in my very soul – kiss the children. Goodbye Darling Precious MBE

Bivouac, below Etowah River, May 21, 1864

My Precious Loving Wife,

Since last letter we have made a slight retrograde movement. We are now bivouacked between the Etowah River and Altoona. Whether we will move backwards, forward or remain stationary I have no means of ascertaining. Even when we are on the march we do not know where we are going – neither do we know at what hour we will take up our line of march – It is just as natural for us to move at night as during the day. Darling I have no news therefore I will be brief this time. On yesterday when we reached this camp I went down to the creek and took a good chunk of soap and had a grand bath. I felt relieved of a load of dirt. I had no clean clothes to put on but then I had clean skin which was some consolation. Darling, I have not heard from you in several days, but the reason is we have had no mail delivered to us. As soon as I have an opportunity I shall hunt up the mail. Love, I shall write to Dr. Houston in a few days reminding him to send that money for Mary's hire to you. Dr. Brewster is here. He came up two or three days ago. I think he is attached to the infirmary Corps. I trust darling, our little boy has recovered his health. I am quite anxious to hear from him. Tell sister I am waiting patiently for her to learn to write that she may write me a letter. Also, let me know if Buddy is learning. I think he might be spelling in two syllables by this time. I hope something may turn up that I may get home by the middle of summer. I was never so anxious to get home, but still I know there is no possible chance. But as I stated in a previous letter I do sincerely hope that better days are not far in the future. If we can only destroy the Yankee army in Georgia I think there will be rest for the weary war worn soldier. Well darling not knowing at what hour we may move I will close I have written in double quick haste and have written much more than I anticipated when I commenced. My love tell Pa to come see me if he can get here. Goodbye my Precious Darling wife & children. Your devoted and loving Husband, MBE

Bivouac, near Etowah River, May 22, 1864

My precious darling wife,

My heart was made to throb with emotions of delight this morning by the timely arrival of two sweet missives from my own true and faithful wife the last one bearing date Monday noon 10th. The other a day or two older. I was in some suspense – not having heard from you in several days – but having had the assurance that you were well _____ able to __________ again, I felt greatly relieved. I am, however, much troubled on account of your ______________ and suspense, I do trust darling you will not give yourself unnecessary trouble on my account or in other words – that you will not anticipate trouble on my account or in other words – that you will not anticipate trouble. You know that sufficient unto the day is the evil thereof. I hear from home and learn that all are well. I have reason to be thankful – You also hear from me and are greeted with the same sense- Therefore we must not look into the future for trouble. I am happy to inform you dearest that I am enjoying robust health, have a splendid appetite – can eat any cornbread without meat and it tastes better than biscuits for my taste. Judson is well. Brother James is not well – but he is with the wagon train where he is not exposed to a hard march & c. George came in yesterday from the hospital at Madison, GA. He was kindly assisted by a gentleman by the name of Hillsman, a cousin of Pa's. George brought a large haversack full of biscuits, ham, sugar, coffee (old fashioned) and I tell you we had a feast. I will not tell you how we hid the good things – but just let you imagine. Well precious wife we've been in the woods about a day and a half resting – Oh! what a blessing rest is to the poor, tired, jaded, foot-sore soldier. On every hill and in every valley can the soldiers be seen – reclining on the ground enjoying the sweet sweet rest – after so many days of forced marches up the hills – through mud, dust & c.-beneath the blazing sun – But we are perfectly fresh this morning and ready to march at a moment's warning. We will probably move this evening but as to the direction – whether north, south, east or west I know there is a man in the know. Our casualty report this morning [The rest of the letter, until the last page, is missing.] that the Yankees are retreating back to Chattanooga – whether this be so or not, I cannot say, but I am satisfied they are not pressing us – or we would not have remained stationary so long. At any rate, I see no prospect of a battle, just at this time, now loved one, don't get low spirited any more. If you do not get my letters just imagine the mails are out of joint or that Gen'l Houston will not suffer any communication with the people at home – fearing that they might be distributed to the service or something of this sort. I have been in some of the tightest sort of places, and have come out all right.

Therefore, beloved, hope for the best and trust that all will be right. I feel assured that there are many happy days of bliss in store for us. God speed that happy period when we will be content to spend the remainder of our lives together in quiet blissful happiness. Darling, don't send me any more paper, I have more than I want, besides I have plenty of envelopes, wish you had some of them.[20]

Bivouac, Mercer's Brigade, May 25, 1864

I have not written in three or four days but I have had no opportunity of course I can snatch a moment at almost any time to write a short note but when we are marching it is a very difficult matter to get a letter mailed. The last letter I wrote –dated I think 22nd was sent down to Atlanta or some other place still lower down to mail – as I had understood that our letters were stopped in Atlanta for the present I do not know for certain that this is the case but to provide against all contingencies I ran the Blockade with the letter above mentioned. Since I wrote last we have made several changes On day before yesterday we marched a few miles south of the old bivouac near Etowah River – On yesterday we made a heavy march – having reached a point about 16 miles from the Chattahoochee and 25 miles from Atlanta This morning we were marched several miles on the backtrack & we were now in Bivouac in the woods a few miles from Dallas – I suppose we are in Cobb or Spaulding County – I do not try to keep the geography of the country. Well darling I have no news. Whether we will get a fight from the Yankees or not. I have no means of ascertaining where the Yankee army is. I suppose some columns are not far from us – as we were turned back this morning. They are trying to avoid a battle hoping to drive us back by flank movements – Your last letter was dated 16th Inst I am very

---

[20] May 18–22 found Johnston's Army near the Etowah River around Altoona Pass. On May 25, Johnston's army met the Union forces at New Hope Church, resulting in a victory for the Confederate forces. Coleman, *A History of Georgia,* 200.

anxious to get news from you. We have had no mail in several days- Bro James is still in the war – I learn he is improving. Judson and George are well- We have had quite a number of our company sick – some 17 I believe- Precious I write in great haste my love to all Kiss Eddy and Lizzie and tell them to kiss Ma for Pa. I will write again soon –in the meantime be cheerful Darling I am quite well – but a little fatigued from marching. Your devoted Husband MBE

Near Dallas, Georgia, May 29, 1864

My Precious Wife,

Yesterday I wrote a short hurried note as the courier was waiting I could do no better. In fact I was so hurried I folded my note and directed it walking along the road with him. Darling I read 3 letters from you on yesterday (the first mail we've had all week) and I had a most pleasant and agreeable time in perusing them. Every line seemed to breathe the deep anxiety for my welfare. I am afraid Darling you give yourself unnecessary concerns on my account. I feel sure that we'll come out all right. In fact, I have always thought so. Your letters Darling which I received on yesterday were dated 26th, 21st, 25th inst I have received 10 or a dozen letters from you since I left Hardeeville. I suppose I have read all you've written. Precious, I am not well – have been quite feeble for several days – I shall go back to the rear until I feel better. My bowels are paining me and I have some fever. Fighting and skirmishing have been going on ____________________ In fact this seems to be a never ending conflict. I feel to bad to write a long letter I will write again Darling tomorrow or next day We have been moving night and day for a long time. But, we have been in this place for over 24 hours & have rested finely. There is some fighting to our right and left but everything is as still as a mouse in front of us – In fact the Yankees never attack our rifle pits until our crowd goes away – We seem to miss it all here of late My love to all – kiss the children. On day before yesterday our boy was five years old – I did not forget it & one month and three days ago our daughter was 8 years of age. But, I must close, have not heard from

Brother James since he left – Judson and George are well Your devoted husband, MBE You must forgive this letter, for I have never felt less like writing

Bivouac, 2 miles south of Dallas, Georgia, May 30, 1864

My Precious Darling Wife

Since my last note we have been stationary & of course we have been resting finely. The Yankees make an occasional charge on our lines – particularly at night. But, they are always repulsed. They made several charges last night on our right also on our left. But, they did not accomplish anything, we are snugly fixed. have extensive breast work and rifle pits and it will put them to some trouble to hurt us. I am not very well. Have a bowel disease. I am feeling very weak this morning. I am still with the Regt. If I get any worse I will go to a Hospital. I have no news I hear but little- hardly ever see any papers. You know more about the army of the Tennessee – provided you read the papers – than I do – We have quite a number of sick – I suppose more than a third of our company is sick. I have not heard from Jimmy since he went to the hospital. Judson and George are well. Love to all. Write by every opportunity Darling. Goodbye my Precious Wife. Your devoted Husband, MBEly

Spring 1864, undated partial letter

(read a portion of this letter to Pa – that about the boys especially)

[2nd page]

But how are you off – for something to eat did you say, Well so so. We had flapjacks and syrup for supper tonight. Sometimes we have biscuits – sometimes dog bread.[21] We have just at this crisis a whole hog, old man Robinson brought it to his son Billy and fortunately Billy is messing with reg. in fact quite a lucky circumstance. But, how is your

[21] "Dog bread" was a name for hardtack, a staple in a soldier's diet.

health at this time – did you say Ah! Never better Weigh 160 lbs. tough as a donkey with the appetite of a vulture. Brother James is looking better than I ever saw him and his health is better than it has ever been. In fact he never grunts. As to Jud, he is alright and that is enough to say of Jud at any time only I will just add that he is one of the best soldiers in the Confederate army without a doubt. In conclusion if this war would just end Oh what a lovely blessing that would be. Darling, my greatest happiness and ambition is to be at home near you dear and the children – God bless you and my dear boy and girl! How hard it is to be separated from you. But I believe this separation will be brief & that we will be united & soon May I realize this before the expiration of '64.

Your devoted husband, MBE

Darling as I am replying to two letters I must try to give you a pretty long letter though I am already out of soap. I suppose I can rattle on for a while and if the letter grows wearisome you can dash it aside for I can assure you that you will lose nothing by this operation having written all that I know of that could possibly entertain you. While I think of it my dear I will just say that I am needing my hat very much. Please have it pressed & send by someone passing. W. Brannon will be at home soon and you can send it by him when he returns. He was very glad to hear that his father was improving. You asked me dear how I was off for socks. My woolen socks and others are thread bare. My boots are gone up spout and my shoes have ripped from heel to toe. My pants have (black ones) departed this life and my uniform pants are in the last stages of consumption. I shall go to bed & wrap up or borrow from some of the boys – are walking around barefooted with their shirt tails out – But summer will soon be on hand and it will be ok

Undated, near Dalton

[First page missing]

Our works many times recently near Dalton but have been repulsed with considerable slaughter. Love there will not be a chance for you to come to see me In fact- no one but soldiers can pass up the road. I hope

Darling Precious Love You know that the separation is hard – yes almost heart wrenching yet darling the experiences of these times demands it & yet we hope there are better days coming when we will part no more on this earth. I often think love that I am supposed to see the end of this war – I want to stay at home and keep you and the dear children in sight – that I may make up for the long sad separation. But you will soon think I'm down hearted if I write in this strain. You must not think so – I am in excellent spirits – In fact nothing disturbs me except my great desire to see you and the precious children. I wish I could write you an interesting letter Precious but my opportunities are very poor so when I commence writing I am listening every minute for the order to "fall in." We change our camp every day and sometimes we are marching and counter marching till midnight, and of course I have slim chances to write – will however write two or three times every week & if you do not hear from me – keep writing. Our letters may be detained at least while the battle is over. Times are very hard at this place or at least to the right of us. I saw pones of cornbread sell for five dollars and biscuits at 3 for a dollar & finally went up to a dollar a piece, eggs at 5 to 10 dollars a dozen, everything else in proportion. Darling you would laugh if you could see us, every fellow does his own cooking as soon as the Division halts you see little fires along the road spring up like magic and every fellow sharpens a stick and broils his meat over the fire & then he takes his "hardtack" (crackers) & makes a meal –takes a swig from his canteen smokes his pipe & then wraps himself in his blankets and forgets all his cares in true nature's sweet repose – balmy sleep. But I must stop – could write in the morning provided I could mail it Kiss the children and give my love to all Goodbye precious darling wife Yours MBEly.

Though there are no surviving letters for June, the 54th was involved in battles in the Atlanta area. There were battles at Kolb's Farm, Kennesaw Mountain, and Pace's Ferry. Sherman's troops were soundly defeated at Kennesaw Mountain. In July, President Davis relieved General Johnston of his command, replacing him with General John Bell Hood. Marcus's brother

James lost his leg on July 22, and there were several casualties from the Russell Guards.[22]

July 3, 1864

My precious Wife,

I have just learned that all the sick which can be removed will be sent to Selma or Montgomery this morning at 1 o'clock, myself among the number. I tried very hard to be left behind but "no go." There is now no chance to see you, when I am discharged from the hospital or rather when I get ready to go back, I will come by home. One of our officers just got in from Macon. He says Bro. James is there & doing very well. Welcome, Welcome, news! When I get to my destination I will write again. My dear you have not written. I have expected a letter for several days. Spent last night at Mrs. McCrory's, they had plenty of rice, peaches and melons. Your devoted, MBEly

Auburn, Alabama, August 11, 1864

My Dearest Love,

I have not heard from you in a long time. I wrote you the day I left Columbus- also – a short time after reaching the hospital at Auburn. I am better placed in many respects with this Hospital – than the Gen Hospital at Columbus – but had much rather be at Columbus on account of being nearer to you. I am not improving at all but having chills - or rather agues every other day. I am quite feeble today but as it is ____ _____ day ________________________________ Love to all Write to me Your affectionate husband, MBEly

Texas Hospital, Auburn, Alabama, August 15, 1864

My Precious Wife,

I have supplied myself with some nice paper and now prepared to write you a long letter in answer to the very interesting one received by

---

[22] Coleman, 200.

this morning's mail. I was indeed very proud and glad to receive your very kind and loving letter because I was so anxious to hear from you and the children as well as Brothers James and Judson. Having enjoyed the happy privilege of knowing everything is as well as I could desire. I feel at least 50 percent better. In fact I was almost afraid to hear from the boys especially brother James. My health is improving a little when I relapsed with chills and fever they alternated for a few days. After ______ I had a chill every day for four days together and then they suddenly left me. Since then I have been improving slowly but am very weak and feeble. On the advice of Dr. Bryan of this Hospital I applied to Dr. B this morning for four days leave of absence to go to Columbus expecting to come home and stretch my four days to a week or more. He refused my application stating that he had received orders forbidding it. But he said he would transfer me to Columbus if I would make application to Dr. Stout which I accordingly did. I felt very badly this morning then the Dr refused to give me a short leave of absence but then I concluded if my furlough failed I might still get a transfer to Columbus or Forsyth. For that reason love I want you to write immediately and state your preference. You see my darling I have been making every effort to make some arrangement to be with you. It seems very hard when I am away from the front that I cannot spend the time with my family. If all my prospects fail there is at least one that will not fail. For when I get my discharge I am coming by home if I have to fight my way through. But you need have no fear that we will be together in Columbus in spite of Dr. Perry and Co.

Near Lovejoy's Station, September 6, 1864

My Darling Wife,

I have had no opportunity to write for several days – I wrote you last as I passed through Griffin at least I did not pass directly through All the men from different hospitals were sent to the camp of ________ & I among the rest. After I had been in Griffin a day and a night I was sent up to the front & placed on the left of our line of battle in this strange crowd. I was very much dissatisfied & disheartened with this arrangement – I was allowed to go my company the next day. I found the boys all well none of them having been killed or wounded in the fight near Jonestown. Cater Huckaby[23] was left sick and supposed to be captured. Last night the Yanks disappeared from our front. The boys went over this morning to their rifle pits & got some of their ________ left behind. No one knows where they are gone. They may have gone back to Atlanta & they may be flanking us most probably the latter. Don't know what will become of our country times are very ____________. Dear send my tent when you have an opportunity also a blanket if you can get one for if I do not get a blanket I will freeze this winter. I am making out miserably as regards to sleeping arrangements. I learn Bro J left for home last Saturday was very glad to hear it. We will move today or tonight when I get to a stopping place will write again. Goodbye love, I write in great haste. Your devoted, MBEly

Camp near Jonesboro, September 12, 1864

My Precious Mattie,

We received mail yesterday for the first since I have been here but I was not a happy sharer in its contents. I hope our mails will be regular in the future as I am getting very anxious to hear from you. What has become of Judson? The time he set to leave is past, long ago - we are now having a season of rest. Genl's Hood & Sherman have agreed upon a ten days truce commencing today in order that the citizens of Atlanta may be removed consequently everything is very quiet – no booming cannons nor whistling minnies – giving everything the appearance of a huge camp meeting. It seems to be the prevailing opinion in the army

---

[23] Cater Huckaby was captured at Jonesboro on August 31, 1864 (see Co. H 54th "The Russell Guards" Biographies). Henderson, *Roster of the Confederate Soldiers,* 5:704.

that this campaign is over. In fact some go so far as to say that the last gun in this war has been discharged but I cannot see why they entertain any such notions. I think the Yankees have received encouragement to provocate the war. It is a current rumor that Gen Beauregard will take command of the army of Tennessee & I learn that he has already arrived. Everyone is busy cleaning his gun & policing the camps – so we may look out for a grand review. How is Bro. James? I saw Dr. Godfrey[24] yesterday and he inquired about him and seemed to be agreeably surprised that he was doing well. He told me that Bro. J fainted under the operation and he had to resort to stimulants to revive him. He also said that he thought at the time he would die – but now the crisis is past. George is well – I am not quite well having a diarrhea that is troublesome. I think this is the sixth letter & although they have no news – still I hope you have rec'd all I have written. If you have an opportunity love send me syrup & butter you can melt the butter and put it in a bottle - our rations are rather slim. Don't forget my tent cloth for you know – having failed to get a blanket I have nothing to cover me at night. I want a pair of boots made. Please see Uncle Tom McLeroy[25] and get him to make them right away. I want them made very high & out of the best material No. 9 – so that I can get them on and off easily. I shall soon be barefoot. Call at the Express Office occasionally to see if Dr. Houston has sent that money. I want to live close so I can send you some more money but as we get only beef enough for one meal each day and no bacon. I am obliged to buy a little rice ($1.00 per pound) and such other little things that I can get. But this is the driest country I ever saw. The Yanks destroyed everything – They even eat up all the old ganders as I

[24] Dr. James Erwin Godfrey amputated James Ely's leg in Atlanta on July 22, 1864. He was the surgeon for the 54th Infantry. Dr. Godfrey practiced medicine before and after the war in Madison (see People and Places). "Dr. J.E. Godfrey," Morgan County Heritage, last modified 2015, http://www.morgan-countyheritage.org/communities/godfrey/document/ dr-je-godfrey.

[25] Thomas McLeroy ("Uncle Tom") was a neighbor of the Ely family and a shoemaker (see People and Places). *1860 U.S. Federal Census, Georgia, Harris County, Cataula Dist.*, 24.

frequently see their heads lying about. All the luxury our boys have is the sugar millet. They go for miles after it and frequently sell it for 25cts a stalk. It does not take them long to fill out a ten acre field of it .I have lost my testament – send me another if you can get one. How are Lizzie and Eddie? I suppose they are getting fat on syrup – Goodbye my love – I must hasty close. I have to go to the inspection of new Company. Devotedly, MBE

In July and August, Sherman's troops managed to cut off the major supply lines of the Confederacy by taking the railroad lines in Northeast Georgia and the Atlanta area. There was fierce fighting in the Atlanta area, resulting in a sound Confederate defeat. Hood withdrew from Atlanta on September 1, burning military supplies and installations. Atlanta was now in Union hands.[26]

Bivouac, 1 mile north of Jonestown, September 14, 1864

My precious wife,

The yesterday's mail brought a letter for me – I was truly glad to hear from you for it has been two weeks since I left and I was getting uneasy – Glad to learn you had rec'd your express receipt – and the only regret I have in regard is that it is not in my power to send you as much every week. We are enjoying the fine pleasant weather & can enjoy on the move on account of the rain and mud that have annoyed us so much recently. The nights are quite cool and frost may be expected in a few weeks. Love, if you could be here for a short season you would not think there was much danger just now – Everything is just as it was in old Beaulieu – and we are daily enacting Beaulieu scenes – that is having reveille, Tattoos, Guard mountings and inspections. I do hope the quiet will continue long enough to give our foes time to reflect on the error of their ways and they will be constrained to go home and have us paddle our own canoe. Your letter dear was written on Monday or Tuesday and

[26] Gallman, *The Civil War Chronicle,* 440.

Bro. James left Griffin on Saturday. It is quite strange he has not reached home. You spoke of the thunder and lightning on the morning to which refer Heard's and Sherman's Artillery was booming away – Strangely mixing & echoing with heaven's artillery – presenting altogether a fierce and awful picture. Dear I have written for so many things recently that I hate to ask for anything more but the shirt you made for me has torn to pieces it is easier to tear than paper. The calico one is all right. This is the dryest country for something to eat I ever saw – I will try to get a 24 hours pass & go to Barnesville to see your Bro W. I think I can get a blanket from your sister.

Write often Your devoted, MBE

Bivouac, 1 mile south of Jonesboro, September 17, 1864

My precious wife,

This is Saturday evening, on this particular evening I was thinking of home and all the blessings it was our invariable custom in day of yore to make all our little arrangements for the coming Sabbath hence my mind always wanders to those happy days. Gen Hardee's troops was reviewed by the Commanding General at Jonesboro today. Everything passed off in grand style. I did not much enjoy the military display as I felt too ______________ my bowels being out of order. Our rations which consist of bread and beef do not agree with me. I crave something good to eat would give $20.00 (if I had it) for a good meal of victuals. But as I cannot get it I try to content myself without. As I am looking for a letter tonight I'll discontinue for the present. It is Sunday morning – It has just ceased raining – commenced at midnight and while I am drying myself by the fire I will finish my letter. We received orders last night to have two days rations cooked. It is therefore likely that we will move in some direction today - perhaps to Newnan. I have just learned that Lee's Corps of this army are on their way to Virginia. Sherman's reinforcing Grant – I do not know that this is true. Darling your letters fail to reach me – I have rec'd but one since I returned & have written seven or eight. I shall not write anymore until I get a letter as I have no envelopes and shall have to depend on turning yours and sending them back. Where is Judson? It is strange he does not return. Am afraid he relapsed. How is Bro J progressing? Wish I could be with you all a few days – Kiss Eddie & Lizzie love to Bro J & sister ____________ and accept a double share from Your devoted husband, MBE

Bivouac, in rear of rifle pits, September 27, 1864

I have written you several letters recently but am fearful they did not reach you. It is therefore necessary to explain again to you that the army is on the Atlanta & West Point R Road a few miles above Palmetto – We reached this place a week ago – have built our works extending from several miles east of the railroad to the Chattahoochee River and beyond as I learn the Pontoon Bridges have been laid down. In addition to the letter Judson brought I received one dated 16th just on yesterday – the first mail we have had in nearly three weeks & now as we have rather an idle day I will write you a long letter if I can possibly think of anything to write – for you have written several long dear letters to me. Yesterday was quite a busy day with us. At 9 o'clock in the morning we drilled. The whole army formed in front of the works about 11 o'clock to receive President Davis who is here on a visit. The President together with Genl's Hood, Hardee &c road <u>past</u> on splendid chargers, bowing and touching their hats and we in return flourished our old hats and yelled like a set of maniacs. Splendid bands were discoursing sweet music all along the line – colors were flying &c – taking all in all we had quite a gala day. But amidst all this pomp and pride and military display a solemn scene was being enacted. A lieutenant of the 63rd Virginia Regt had deserted his country's flag He was arrested tried & condemned to be shot with muskets at 11 o'clock am 26th and while the army was shouting a welcome to President Davis – the fearful sentence was enacted. The way of the transgressors is hard. Dear since I received my tent and blanket I have a very comfortable time. Lt. Land & I have forks driven in the ground and split poles for plank to sleep on. We then have it covered over with leaves and a blanket laid on & one also to cover with. We then have the tent stretched over our bed and you can't imagine how comfortable we are. It is true we have hard sleeping but good enough for a soldier. Lt. Land has a mule and when we are on a march we can carry all our things on this mule which is very convenient. President Davis says the Yankees must be driven from the soil of Ga & that speedily. Well I reckon he sees how this thing can be accomplished but I must confess I do not. In the first place our army is deserting by hundreds & if something is not done we will soon be a mere remnant of any army. I think there will be many more deserters shot this fall. If our country was truth itself we would not now have a large Yankee Army at our very door. But there are so many miserable cowards shirking out of this war – that a mere hand full is left. Those miscreants have no idea of baring their breasts to the bullets. I do not know where such characters will go to for old Satan will have no use for them. How do the __________ get on saving their __________. they are such a sweet set of mortals. Joe Brown & Bro James on furlough. Jud is well – George complaining. I am going off today to hunt some ______________

Your devoted MBE Kiss the children Love to all[27]

On the road, west of the Chattahoochee River, September 30, 1864

Darling Wife, While we are resting I will write a line & trust to chance to mail it on the road. We broke up camp yesterday morning and moved in the direction of Palmetto at that place we changed our course due west. Last night we bivouacked on the west bank of the Chattahoochee This morning crossed over and we are now waiting till the different wagon trains pass us then we will take up our line of march.

---

[27] Colonel Charles Olmstead also wrote about President Davis's visit to Palmetto in his memoirs: "President Davis visited the army while we were at Palmetto. I caught sight of him as he galloped along our brigade front – a white faced haggard looking man, burdened down – I imagined at the time – by the cares and responsibilities that were upon him." Lilla Mills Hawes, ed., *The Memoirs of Charles H. Olmstead* (Atlanta GA: The Georgia Historical Society, 1964) 158.

By reference to the map you will see Carroll County north of Heard – The county seat is Carrollton. We will probably pass through this town & through Haralson County on to Ala. Don't know certainty where we are moving to Blue Mountain, north Ala or middle Tennessee. I am afraid Darling our correspondence for some time will cease as the mail arrangements may be cut off. But be assured dear that I will take every advantage to write. The weather is warm We are feeling __________.

Goodbye, your Devoted MBEly

Gadsden, Alabama, October 22, 1864

Darling Wife,

I wrote you a long letter on yesterday. I write again this morning to inform you certainly of our destination. We take up our line of march for Tennessee this morning - That point is settled – all doubt removed. Last night there was a perfect Jubilee in Gadsden. Genl's Beauregard, Cheatham, Wood, Butts and all the generals were serenaded by the different bands & of course all made speeches. We take up our line of march according to the programme today. When we get to Tennessee we expect to whip Sherman and wrest Tennessee from the Yanks and establish our independence. Sacrifices must be made - every man must do his duty & and his whole duty and the victory is ours – I am sorry to be so far away from my dear beloved precious family – those who are dearer to me than life – but I am now well assured that this move will end the war very soon in our favor and then all can spend the remainder of their lives with their families in peace & happiness – may God speed the time. Write darling when you can. I wish to hear from you often & I hope the mail route will remain open. Goodbye Precious. Kiss the children & love to all Your devoted, MBE

Tuscumbia, Alabama, November 1, 1864, Bivouac, South Bank, Tennessee River

My Precious Wife,

Some days have elapsed since I wrote you – for want of an opportunity. When at Gadsden I wrote two letters. We left there about ten days ago & no opportunity has presented itself for sending off a mail up to this date. I will endeavor to give you a short account of our march since we left Gadsden & it should appear a little gloomy we will laugh at it and consider it a soldier's lot. Not to be particular about dates-we left Gadsden about ten days ago moving north. We were three days __________ ____________ Sand Mountain. On the fourth night we marched nearly all night in the darkness was such that we scattered in every direction. We finally stopped & pitched our camp in a swamp – The rain fell rapidly I struck my tent and went to sleep – Soon there was a perfect sheet of water – all over the swamp and of course we had to rise from our wet beds and roost like chickens. I split up a rail and made a scaffold & got up on it and snatched a few short naps during the night. Besides the unpleasantness of our situation we had no rations. The next morning we crawled out and minded up our fires to dry – I put off and had the good fortune to get a breakfast at a house close by. About noon we moved up towards Decatur a town strongly fortified by the Yankees. We surrounded the town during the night & skirmishing commenced in good earnest. I went to sleep that night & still no rations – confident that we would storm this fort in Decatur. The next morning we could see the hated Yankee flags floating defiantly the emblem of Yankee tyranny & oppression We knew that this place surrounded with ditches & a strong network of wire where they had destroyed the telegraph would be as impregnable as Gibraltor but we were hungry and we were willing to fight for our bellies as well as our country – The morning sun rose clear & bright but no order came to advance on the town – I think Gen Hood concluded that the sacrifice would be too great. We therefore & ______________ sharp skirmishes & artillery duels were going on through the day. That evening I paid a Dollar for a quart of meal & it unsifted. I divided it among five or six I thought it the best bread I ever tasted At night our ration came – yes it came & what do you suppose it was – two nubbins of corn to the man & then we got no fodder We parched our corn and eat the last grain We left Decatur the next day going west the first night we [unfinished]

Camp near Tuscumbia, November 21, 1864

My Precious Wife,

The mail carrier has just come from _______________ without the mail. I was expecting mail from home and it was expected to be sent to Cherokee the __________ terminus of the Railroad. From Corinth Mississippi the mail courier will go back tomorrow to try again for the mail. I could prepare a few lines to send off our opportunity for mailing letters are few and I take advantage of every one. I have nothing to write having written yesterday. We are lying quietly in our bivouac enjoying a season of rest. The weather is rather inclement – cool & cloudy with an occasional shower of rain. But we have plenty of fire wood and keep comfortable. I hear a camp rumor that we will remain at this camp several days. But there is no reliance in these rumors we may leave tomorrow or next day. I wrote yesterday that Lt. Hunter Co. F was dead. This turned out to be a false rumor though he has been quite sick. I have just been practicing a little with the needle. The seat of my pants is nearly or quite threadbare. I tacked on a piece of cloth on the inside as big as a bread box. Besides I darned my socks with black thread and now I am quite respectable. I think we will go into winter quarters in three or four weeks somewhere. I am anxious for the time to come round as I expect to come home after clothing, bedding &c for my company and if that arrangement fails I will get off if possible on a furlough. But sufficient to the day &c should be considered I trust I may have frequent opportunities to write in the future and especially that I may get letters from home regularly. Kiss the children and tell them not to forget Pa – Love to sister Pa & all the rest. The boys are well. I wish I was with you now. It seems I could enjoy more than ever in my life the comforts & joys of home. Goodbye sweet wife & children MBE

Near Cheatham's Ferry, November 23, 1864

My Precious Wife,

Since I last wrote we have left the vicinity of Florence & moved about 18 miles down the river – I mean our Brigade – for the rest of the army has moved towards Nashville for three days. Our camp is opposite Cherokee Station the present terminus of the Rail Road. We have probably been sent down to this post to guard a supply train to the Army at least that is the supposition.

We will remain here 2 or 3 days The mail came in yesterday but brought me no letters I will look again & I hope with better success next time. The weather is ________________ There was snow on day before yesterday – some of us are thrilled – but we are after Yankees now and don't have time to think about cold weather. We are getting plenty to eat now We draw bacon beef hard bread and sometimes flour. We have no cause to complain. I only wish I could hold you darling & kiss the dear children & both hold on.

(This is all the paper I have Kiss the children)

After the fall of Atlanta, Sherman and Hood agreed on a ten-day armistice. The Confederate Army was reorganized and the 54th Regiment was placed in Cleburne's division after the death of General Walker during the Atlanta Campaign. September found the troops moving toward Dallas, Georgia and then to Lovejoy's Station. The end of October found the 54th in Carroll County, getting ready to move into northern Alabama. They marched to Tuscumbia, Alabama, crossed the Tennessee River, and continued toward Nashville. They moved on toward Murfreesboro and then back to Franklin, Tennessee. According to Aaron Land in his war memoir, the 54th marched from Murfreesboro back to Franklin (a distance of 75 miles) in one day. [28]

---

[28] Simmons, *A Concise Encyclopedia of the Civil War*, 218–20.

1865

"I Long to Be at Home"

Officer's Hospital, Uniontown, Alabama, January 21, 1865

Most Precious Wife,

I have written you two short letters recently, informing you I was once more an inmate of a hospital I reached this place two or three days ago _ have been quite feeble ever since my arrival – having kept my bed nearly all the time – But I am better this morning. My bowels seem to move quite well but my cough is still very bad. The Doctor told me on yesterday that he would furlough me as soon as I was able to travel I shall be able to go before the board in a week. This is the best conducted hospital I ever saw. In fact it is said to be the best in the CS. The hospital is in a large hotel. The place is everything the most fastidious appetite could crave far surpassing any hotel in my knowledge. We get toast, biscuit, batter cake & bread – eggs – butter - chicken – tea coffee with milk & sugar &C &c for Breakfast & supper Besides everything for Dinner including Slice Potato Pie. I am not well enough to enjoy all these edibles but will do them ample justice soon I am very anxious to hear from home darling – have not heard in several weeks. There are letters for me doubtless back at the command Devotedly MBE

Officer's Hospital, Uniontown, Alabama, January 25, 1865

My Precious Wife

I wish it were in my power to write you a long letter; but so it is- I am too feeble_ my strength will not permit. On yesterday I expected to go before the board _ but was disappointed _ for at breakfast I was attacked with veralgia of the kidneys_ I was in a perfect agony of pain for several hours_ In fact it seemed that nature could endure no more – The

Doctor cupped me[1] – applied pepper poultices[2] – administered morphine all to no purpose_ At last he gave me a dose of powerful medicine which gave me almost instant relief & such a relief _ It seemed as if I had entered a new world of existence – I dropped into a profound sleep & this morning finds me quite feeble but free from pain _ The board meets again in a few days will go before it. Love Darling for yourself & children Yours MBE

Officer's Hospital, Uniontown, Alabama, January 27, 1865

My Precious Wife

Feeling "tolerably well" this morning. I have concluded to write you a lengthier note than usual – not that I have any real good news "or anything of the kind" as Billy Brown says – but merely to show my willingness to write at length _ health & strength per willing Well as to my situation _ am quite feeble – bowels disordered – have occasional fevers – but suffering no pain. I asked the Doctor yesterday to let me go before the board which meets today – He refused stating that I was not well enough _ but as soon as my health improved – he would give me sixty days & that by waiting & getting my furlough improved I could enjoy it more &c&c. If I should get a leave of absence by the middle or 20th of Feby _ I can remain at home till the same time in April & see to our little farm & many other things. There will be no difficulty in getting the furlough sooner or later _ It depends all together on my improvement & I shall endeavor to be very careful of my health. I long to be at home sweet home once more with my wife & little ones. I am treated kindly get plenty to eat _ but still want some of our old fashioned waffles. Yours MBE Kiss the children

---

[1] When "cupping," physicians would heat small glass cups and place them on the skin to create a vacuum, which drew blood to the area to form a blister. Schroeder-Lein, 248.

[2] Pepper poultices were made from peppers such as cayenne and used to draw infection, treat boils and abscesses, and relieve inflammation or a rash. Ibid., 76.

Uniontown, Alabama, February 1, 1865

My Precious Wife

There seems to be some mystery I can not unravel for it is passing strange that I can not hear one word from home. I have looked – but looked in vain for a letter. I know you are not to blame love for judging from your precious punctuality – I am very uneasy – but still I trust there is nothing wrong – except the mails _ I suppose the boys are at home as I heard all the Georgia Troops were to be disbanded for 8 or 10 days – When I first received this news – I felt very sad that I could not be with them to enjoy the furlough. But I hope soon to spend a long one at home as there has been a sick furlough of 60 days sent up for me. I suppose it will be the middle of the month before it gets back to me. Love it makes me feel mighty proud that I will soon – perhaps have the pleasure of spending 2 months at home. I am not quite so well off today – have had a very bad boil on my breast_ also my bowels are not right But I shall live light & hope to get better soon. I may have a chance of sending this as far as Columbus by someone passing. Your Devoted Husband MBE Kiss the children

Uniontown, Alabama, February 4, 1865

My Precious Wife

It is very strange and unaccountable that I receive no tidings from you. I think it must be nearly three weeks ago that I wrote notifying you that I was on my way to the hospital at Uniontown, Ala. I know love it has been no fault of yours but something wrong with the mails. I have written you at least 8 or 10 letters recently. Fearing almost to hear from you as it has been nearly two months since I heard I shall write to Pa today also My health is still quite feeble _ I am up and down sometimes have fever I am very inactive yet _ I am walking around with much interest in getting my 60 day furlough. Thinking I will improve faster when I get home. Kiss the children Your devoted husband MBEly

Walker Hospital, Columbus, March 22, 1865

Precious Dear Wife

I write you a short note this morning I may be improving – a little – Everybody says I look better & if that be the case – if it follows – that I should feel better . My Uniontown papers are a failure I must give up all hope of seeing them since they have been gone seven weeks, my papers from this hospital have been gone a week. Sister _Cousin Nancy Odom & Millie Ely have been to see me – brought 2 doz. Eggs &c I am keen as a razor to get home – but see no more immediate prospects

Your MBE

Columbus, March 28, 1865

My Precious Wife

I received your letter & the shoes yesterday from Mr. Jackson I was delighted to hear from home. I wish I could get news from home every day. It seems that I am more anxious than ever to get home. The Hospital is a very tiresome place to me. I had almost as soon be in the county jail. My health is improving I think – My bowels are in better condition than they have been in – in a long time. But I do not think my discourse of the chest improves. I have a very severe pain in my left lung and back & shoulder nearly all the time. But I am not suffering much with it this morning. I am gaining a little flesh I hope to be well enough to enjoy my… [rest of letter missing]

April 1865 found Marcus Ely back in the hospital in Macon, Georgia with a diagnosis of phthisis (tuberculosis or consumption). His last service record indicated he was released on April 28, 1865.

Ely and Dumas Family Biographies

The Ely Family

I started searching for my ancestors in the late 1970s, before the age of the internet or computers. My great aunt Esther Blakeley Klutts sent me a dilapidated family Bible that belonged to Moses Dumas. (It's a miracle this Bible has survived, as it went through the 1928 Lake Okechobee Hurricane in Moorehaven, Florida.) She told me that the Bible belonged to my great-great-great-grandfather Moses Dumas. Thus began my search for family roots. The gift of the letters written by my great-great-grandfather began my in-depth research into the Eley (Ely) family.

Osborn Ely — Jesse Eley, the son of Samuel Eley and Mary Jordan Hillsman, settled in Greene County, Georgia after the Revolutionary War. He married Nancy Haynes Shackleford, the daughter of Captain Parmenas Haynes, a Revolutionary War soldier from Virginia. They settled in the southeastern part of Greene County purchasing land on the Little River. Jesse and Nancy Eley had six sons and one daughter.

Their son, Osborn Ely, a teacher in the Greene County Poor School, married Adjaline Birdsong in Oglethorpe County, Georgia on February 25, 1828. (Their union resulted in the births of Ann in 1830, Marcus in 1831, James in 1833, Sarah in 1836, Richard in 1839, and Judson in 1840.) Church records in Greene County, Georgia reveal that the Elys had migrated from Green County in the 1830s to Columbus, at that time a frontier town. They settled in the northeast part of the newly formed Muscogee County. The records of Bethel Baptist Church show Osborn Ely, Seaborn Ely, and Wellborn Ely as members. Osborn is also mentioned in Martin's History of Columbus as a member of the school committee. Looking at records in Randolph County, Georgia, Osborn had a farm in the area in the 1840s. However, the family remained in the Columbus area because the deeds stated "Osborn Ely of Muscogee County." Several newspaper articles were found in the *Columbus Ledger-*

Enquirer concerning runaway slaves seen in the vicinity of Osborn Ely's farm in Fort Gaines, Georgia. Osborn's wife, Adjaline died in Randolph on October 6, 1843. Her death notice was recorded in the *Christian Index*. Osborn married Jane Russell on August 18, 1844 in Muscogee County. The Russell family were also members of Bethel Baptist Church and probably lived near the church.

In the late 1840s the Ely family moved to the Cataula area of Harris County. The 1850 census shows Osborn and Jane, along with Marcus (18), James (16), Sarah (14), Richard (11), Judson (10), George (4), and Lucy (0). An infant, Charles Carroll, was born in November 1848 and died eleven months later on October 5, 1849. By 1860, Osborn and Jane had added Robert (8), Ida (6), Fanny (4), and Osborn (0) to their family. Osborn Ely died in Harris County on May 19, 1869.

Marcus Bethune Ely — Marcus was born on December 2, 1831 in Greene County, Georgia. Marcus attended and graduated from Brownwood Institute (LaGrange) in 1850 and became a teacher. He met Martha Frances Dumas ("Mattie"), also a teacher. (Mattie attended LaGrange Female College and graduated in 1854.) Marcus and Mattie married on May 1, 1855 in Barnesville, Georgia. After their marriage, Marcus and Mattie moved to Ft. Gaines, Georgia, where Marcus taught school. Their first child, Elizabeth Birdsong Ely (Lizzie), was born on April 25, 1856, followed by Edwin Dumas Ely ("Eddie"), born May 27, 1859. I found letters written by Mattie's brother Jerry to the couple during this time. Mattie and Jerry were the youngest children of Moses and Frances Hendley Dumas. During the time the couple lived in Ft. Gaines, Marcus and Jerry planned to start a business together in Ft. Gaines; unfortunately, the precarious times prevented the venture from coming to fruition.

Marcus enlisted in Co. H, 54th Regiment, in Columbus on May 12, 1862. It is interesting to note that the "Russell Guards" was formed by Charles R. Russell, the brother of Marcus's stepmother, Jane. Marcus immediately left for the Savannah area with many of the men in his unit who had enlisted on the same day.

After the war, Marcus and Mattie settled back in Harris County, and for a short time Marcus farmed, but by the 1870s, he was establishing schools in Phenix City, Alabama and surrounding areas. Their third child, Lucy Osborn Ely, was born January 8, 1867. Marcus and Mattie joined the First Baptist Church in Phenix City in 1873. Elizabeth, the oldest daughter of the Elys, married Abram Blakeley, a machinist from Chester, Pennsylvania, on October 13, 1878.

Marcus became Superintendent for the Girard Public School System (Phenix City) for several years in the 1870s. He served as principal of Brownville Public School in 1878. In 1879, Marcus went back to the Columbus area to teach. He died at his home on April 5, 1880 and was buried in Linwood Cemetery. After his death Mattie and Lizzie continued to teach in the Browneville, Alabama area. On July 19, 1881 Eddie died of typhoid fever in Browneville. He was 22 years of age. His obituary stated that he was a young man of promise and good disposition. Eddie was buried in the family plot in Linwood Cemetery.

Tragically, in September 1886, Lucy, the youngest child of the Elys, died unexpectedly during a visit to an aunt living in Atlanta. Her obituary stated that her body was met by her uncle, George W. Ely, in Opelika. She was also buried in the Linwood family plot. Among the pallbearers were Albert Kirven (a prominent Columbus businessman) and Charles Russell. She was laid to rest September 25, 1886.

The 1880 census found Mattie living in the community of Nances in Muscogee County with Marcus's brother James, also a teacher. Some of her neighbors included Samuel Rodgers and Aaron Land, who were in the same unit as Marcus during the Civil War. In the 1900 census, Mattie was living with her daughter Elizabeth in Nances. Abram was a master machinist for Swift Textiles. By 1910, the family had relocated to Woodbury. Abram died January 24, 1912 and is buried in the Woodbury Cemetery. Mattie moved to Woodbury to live with the Blakeleys, where she died on January 1, 1924. She is buried in the Woodbury City Cemetery. Elizabeth died on January 18, 1936 and is also buried in the Woodbury City Cemetery.

James D. Ely — James was born in 1836 in Greene County, Georgia, the second son of Osborn and Adjaline Birdsong Ely. He enlisted in the Russell Guards on August 12, 1862. James lost his right leg (below the knee) during the Battle of Atlanta on July 22, 1864. During the battle, a mini ball went through James's leg right below the knee, resulting in an amputation. After the war, James taught school and was elected as the Harris County Tax Collector. In 1880, after Marcus died, James moved in with Mattie Dumas (Nances Community, Muscogee County). James died in October 1892 and is buried in the Hamilton City Cemetery in Hamilton, Georgia.

Adoniriam Judson Ely — Adoniriam "Judson" Ely was the son of Osborn and Adjaline Ely. He was born October 20, 1840 in Columbus. Judson enlisted in Co. E, Georgia 46th Regiment on March 4, 1862. He transferred to Co. H, 54th Regiment in December. Later that month, he was promoted to 2nd Corporal and then to Sergeant. He remained with Co. H until the end of the war.

Judson married Harriet Newell Brooks on January 17, 1867 in Houston County, Georgia. They had five children: Clifton, Maggie, Sally, Annie Ida, and Jimmie. Between 1880 and 1900, Judson and his family moved to Woodbury. He worked as a carpenter and Hattie taught school. By 1910 Judson was unable to work. His pension application stated that he was suffering from kidney and bladder problems. He died January 26, 1911 and is buried in the Woodbury City Cemetery.

George Wilborn Ely — George was born December 25, 1846 to Osborn and his second wife, Jane Russell. George enlisted as a private in Co. C, 46th Georgia Regiment on April 16, 1862. He was discharged, being under-aged, at Charleston, South Carolina on October 13, 1862. He reenlisted as a private in Barnwell's Battery, Georgia Light Artillery on March 1, 1864. He transferred to Daniell's Battery, Georgia Light Artillery on March 29, 1864. On March 29, 1864 he transferred to Co. H, 54th Georgia Infantry to join his brothers. He surrendered at Greensboro, North Carolina on April 26, 1865.

George married Catherine Stephenson (Talbotton, Georgia) on January 2, 1879. (They had three children: John, Ida, and Clara.) In 1870 the family moved to Corsicanna, Navarro, Texas, and George found employment with the Engineer Corps of the Houston and Texas Central Railroad. He moved up in the ranks of the railroad until he became the traveling passenger agent of the railroad and relocated to Montgomery, Alabama. George was very active in Confederacy organizations after the war. He was a member of the First Baptist Church of Montgomery. In accounts in Columbus newspapers, George made frequent visits to the city.

In an interview he told of his experiences in the Civil War. He tried to enlist several times from 1862 onward. He finally enlisted in the Russell Guards as a private and remained with the unit until the end of the war. At the age of 70, George was still employed by the railroad, but was given a new title: traveling passenger agent on special solicitation only.

In 1910, he was involved in an altercation with his son-in-law involving a pistol. The gun discharged accidentally and George was shot in the leg. The bullet traveled through his knee, shattering it and his lower leg. He was unable to walk for a time, but recovered. George died at his home after a short illness on November 8, 1917. He is buried in Greenwood Cemetery in Montgomery, Alabama.

The Dumas Family

Moses Dumas — Moses was born September 19, 1787, the son of Benjamin and Susannah Hutchins Dumas, in Richmond, North Carolina. He married Frances Hendley on March 12, 1809.They had eight sons and five daughters. By 1830, the Dumas family had settled into Monroe County, Georgia. They lived in the Johnstonville community. Frances Hendley Dumas died July 4, 1849. Moses married Lucretia Buckner on March 7, 1850. Moses died in September 1862. His burial place is unknown.

Jeremiah Jackson Dumas — Though Jeremiah ("Jerry") Dumas was not a part of Marcus Ely's unit, he is an integral part of this story. He and Mattie were the youngest children of Moses and Frances Dumas. Soon after Marcus enlisted and traveled to Beaulieu at Savannah, he received news that Jerry's wife had died. As I transcribed the letters from 1862, I read this piece of information with surprise. In all of the research and information gathered on the Dumas family, this information had never been revealed. As I continued to transcribe the 1862 letters, I read that Jerry had died. I immediately began to try and find out what had happened to Jerry and his wife.

Along with the Civil War letters I had received, there were many letters from other members of the family. I found several letters Jerry had written to Marcus and Mattie and even one that he had written to his father. Several of the letters were written before the Civil War. Jerry worked for grocers George and James Thompson in Perry, Georgia. Though only 21, Jerry was an ambitious young man. In letters written from 1860 to 1862, he revealed his plans and hopes for the future with continuing worries about the political battles between the Northern and Southern states.

While he was working as a clerk, he had stated in an 1860 letter to Mattie and Mark (Marcus) that he was planning to go to Ft. Gaines and go into the grocery business with Mark. (Mark and Mattie were living in Ft. Gaines and Mark was teaching school.) Probably because of the uncertainty of the times, this venture never got off the ground. Jerry continued to live and work in Perry and, in a letter dated June 19, 1861, Jerry wrote,

I can not write you a lengthy letter this morning and a little to each will be included in one as my time is entirely occupied with my business together with the arrangements I am making arrangements for my marriage and from experience you both can very well imagine my condition. I would be delighted if I could have some of my relatives present at the time but I suppose it will be inconvenient besides we are most satisfied owing to the times at having to go to the unnecessary expense of providing refreshments for a large collection. We therefore concluded that we would be married in the morning on the 27th inst having only a few of her nearest relatives to witness ceremony. The name of the "fair creature" destined to be my companion through the "journey of life" is Jeanette Iola Pope. She has been unfortunate in having to give up both of her parents. She has one brother and three or four sisters - the family is of high standing in society – what might be termed "the first circle" A description I believe I gave when I first informed you of the fact. She will doubtless prove to be all that I could wish in fulfilling the duties of a loving and faithful wife. I have not yet enlisted for the war, but I find the temptation hard to resist.

In another letter dated June 24, 1862, he wrote

My furlough will be out next Sunday and I must "away to camps" you may be somewhat surprised to hear me say that I am going to camp= but I know have nothing that bind me to stay any longer at home= After visiting you my wife continued to grow worse and on the 20th she died and her happy spirit winged its flight to realms of eternal bliss where it will ever be at rest= She died so happy! Praying to God that she might receive her soul= Yes she was ____________ Christian= My dear sister – this is a dreadful bereavement indeed! May I have your sympathy and your prayers that I better be able to bear this dreadful trial.

Jerry had enlisted as a private in Co. A, 14th Battalion, Georgia Volunteers on April 26, 1862. After Jeanette's death he rejoined his unit in Calhoun, Georgia. I found a letter (dated July 30, 1862) he had written to his father, Moses Dumas, in which he stated,

I have for some weeks past intended writing you but somehow there has always been something to prevent my doing so= I have been sick with the measles for over two weeks and a pretty severe time I have had. I luckily got permission to stay at a private house where I received kind attention and am free from expense which is very important when you have the measles=I am improving slowly and hope by being prudent I will be well enough to return to camps in a week – all I need is time sufficient to recover my strength.

He also wrote Mattie on the same day,

> I have promised myself often that I would write you though I have been absent only a little over one month. There is nothing at all of interest that I can think to write, But I naturally concluded that you felt some anxiety of mind in regard to my health, whereabouts &c_ Well my sister we are in a portion of the world that might not suit a poet very well but as I haven't a poetical turn of mind I can't say that I am over delighted with the = we are quartered among the hills and mountains remote from civilization where we can hear nothing= neither can we see anything= The inhabitants are all poor but some of them are very kind. I have been very sick with the measles for over two weeks. I am not yet able to do duty but am mending slowly= I fortunately succeeded in getting a room at a private house there the measles first broke out and I have been careful ever since not to expose myself and I think in a week or so I will be able to return to camp= You must excuse a short letter as I have bearly time to get this letter off- I will write again as soon as I can hear from you and will probably have something more interesting to write you.

In Civil War records, it was recorded that Jerry Dumas died on August 30, 1862 at Camp Randolph in Gordon County, Georgia. I kept searching for letters and I found this one,

> Dear Mrs. Ely I received yours the next day after my arrival home and have tried to answer it once before, but was unable to do so. I have been confined to my bed ever since I returned home with Typhoid fever. I write this in bed propped up with a chair and pillows. I am improving slowly and hope to be up soon. I

would like to give you a full detail of your brother's sickness and death but I feel unable to do so in this. But I say to you in relation to his last hours my impression is that he had a triumphant death. The nearer death approached him the happier he appeared. When I get ready to go back to my company I will try to spend a day with you as I suppose you want to hear a full account of his sickness. Yours truly, T.J. Graves.

I was so amazed that I had in my possession letters over 150 years old that had solved this mystery. Fast forward to July 2012, looking on findagrave.com, I found Jeanette and Jerry's graves. They were buried in the old Perry City cemetery. I traveled to the cemetery and found their graves, along with the tiny grave of their infant. I can only suppose that Jeanette died in childbirth along with the baby.

Co. H 54th "The Russell Guards" Biographies

In obtaining information of the men in the 54th Co. H Georgia Volunteers, I searched census records, newspapers, pension records, and Civil War lists. I have searched for and visited as many graves as possible in my pursuit of these men and what happened to them after the war. As you read through the letters, you will read about the daily life of a soldier.

Suffering from lice and fleas, not to mention the insects prevalent along the Georgia coast line, was a constant nuisance. Measles and typhoid fever were a constant threat. During the first years of the conflict, the Russell Guards had enough to eat; families sent and brought food on a regular basis. Wives and other family members visited often. They were involved in only minor skirmishes. Their luck took a sharp turn when they boarded trains and ended up in Dalton. The next two years found the men suffering from hunger, cold, fatigue, and illness. The forced marches were extremely hard, even for the younger soldiers. You can feel the loss of friends, the fear of battle, and the utter loneliness and longing for home.

The years following the Civil War were extremely hard on them and their families. They suffered the aftereffects of their wounds and economic hardships were rampant. Many of them survived and lived long lives. Many of the men remained friends long after the Civil War and were witnesses for them in their Confederate pension applications. Many of the men belonged to Camp Benning Confederate Veterans Organization. They met often and traveled to battle sites for reunions. The Columbus newspapers carried many stories about their activities.

Elias Alverson — Elias Alverson was born in 1840 in Harris County to Moses and May Alverson. He enlisted on November 8, 1862 in Columbus as a private. He married Mildred Smith on May 11, 1864 in Harris County. Elias surrendered with the rest of Co. H in Bentonville, North Carolina in April 1865. After the war, Elias became a farmer and he and Mildred had three sons and three daughters. He lived in Harris County until 1900 when he and Mildred moved to Woodbury. He filed for a pension in 1900 stating that he suffered from heart disease and rheumatism. He owned no property and was destitute. Elias died on June 12, 1908 and is buried in Barnes Cemetery on Cedar Rock Road in Meriwether County, Georgia.

William Ansley — William Ansley was born on January 1, 1832. He was the great-grandson of Thomas Ansley, a Revolutionary War soldier from New Jersey who settled in Warren County, Georgia in 1785 and built the "Rock House," one of the oldest intact homes in Georgia. (Thomas Ansley is also the ancestor of President Jimmy Carter.) William enlisted in Muscogee County on May 20, 1862 as a private. After the war, William became a farmer and married Victoria Dorsey in 1872. They had three sons and three daughters and lived in McDuffie County. He applied for a pension in 1899, stating that he was suffering from rheumatism and shortness of breath. His estimated worth was $10 in household furniture. William died in Boneville, Georgia (McDuffie County) on August 2, 1903.

John P. Arrow — John P. Arrow enlisted as a private on November 8, 1862. No further records found.

Joseph Ashfield — Joseph Ashfield was born on August 5, 1831 in Putnam County, Georgia. He was the son of Joseph and Mary Ashfield. By 1860 he was living in Muscogee County. He married Harriet Frances Spear in Harris County on February 27, 1861. (Harriet was the sister of James Spear, who also served in this unit.) He enlisted on December 5, 1862. At the end of the war he was being treated for frostbite at a military hospital in Augusta, Georgia. He lived and farmed in Harris County until 1898. He and his wife moved to Talbot County, Georgia and lived with Harriet's mother. In his 1900 pension he stated that he was suffering from Bright's disease (kidney) and injury to his right ankle. He owned nothing in 1900; he had owned 40 acres in Harris County, but was forced to sell to pay debts. Joseph died on June 10, 1902 in Talbot County.

John Tyler Attaway — John Tyler Attaway was born in Madison (Morgan County) on November 23, 1844. By 1860, his family had moved to Tallapoosa County, Alabama. (His mother was the head of the family and a farmer. Their real estate was valued at $5,000 and personal property was valued at $9, 395.) He enlisted in Hardeeville, South Carolina in 1862 and stayed with the unit until the close of the war. In his Alabama pension record he stated that he participated in the Battle of Peachtree Creek. John married Mary Elizabeth Hayes in Cusetta, Georgia in 1867. John was a farmer and, by 1880, the family had moved to Alabama and were farming. They had three sons and three daughters. John died in Ozark, Alabama (Dale County) on July 11, 1922 and is buried in the Pleasant Ridge Cemetery in Ozark (the community of Arguta).

James Avant — James Avant was born in Columbus (Muscogee County) in 1837. His parents were Albright and Mary Avant. He enlisted in the unit on November 10, 1862. He was a teamster in the Quartermaster Department. No further records were found.

C. J. Bates — C. J. Bates enlisted as a private on November 10, 1862. He was later detailed to the Pioneer Corps (these troops built roads, bridges, etc.). No further records found.

I. Bazemore — I. Bazemore enlisted as a private on November 10, 1862. No further records found.

Robert F. Beal — Robert F. Beal was the nephew of Margaret Beal Brewster, the wife of Dr. Brewster. He enlisted on May 12, 1862. On January 16, 1863 he was discharged and furnished George T. Pigg as a substitute. He is buried in the Hamilton Cemetery.

John K. Bedell — John K. Bedell enlisted as a 2nd Lieutenant on May 12, 1862. He was elected 1st Lieutenant on December 15, 1863. Lt. Bedell is mentioned in *Charlotte's Boys, Civil War Letters of the Branch Family of Savannah*. On November 7, 1864, Hamilton Branch wrote his mother telling her that they were in Tuscumbia, Alabama, and that he found some of his friends (James Williamson, William F. May, Capt. James Lachlison, and Lt. John K. Bedell) and they were all well. Before the war, John had been in the mercantile business with his family. According to his obituary, John died in Eatonton, Georgia on October 31, 1872. He was 38 at the time. The obituary also stated that he had a frank and generous nature with many friends.

Henry H. Blackmon — Henry H. Blackmon enlisted as a private on May 12, 1862. He transferred to Co. E, 46th Georgia Regt. on December 15, 1862. He surrendered at Greensboro, North Carolina on April 26, 1865.

Levi S. Blake — Levi S. Blake enlisted in Co. I, 20th Reg. on May 23, 1861. He was discharged on disability in Richmond, Virginia on June 23, 1861. He reenlisted on July 26, 1861 and was discharged again with disability on November 1, 1861. He enlisted as a private on January 28, 1863. The roll on February 28, 1864 shows him present. No further records found.

Thomas Bolan — Thomas Bolan enlisted on May 12, 1862. No further records found.

Charles C. Bonnard — Charles C. Bonnard enlisted as a private on October 5, 1862. In December he became an orderly for Colonel Charlton H. Way. Charles was captured at Dalton on October 14, 1864. He was sent to Camp Douglas, Illinois and discharged there on June 17, 1865.

Cornelius Bowles — Cornelius Bowles was born in Georgia in 1825. He married Sarah Roberts in Harris County on November 7, 1848. He enlisted on November 5, 1862. After the war Cornelius and his family tried farming in Harris County, but by 1880 the family had relocated to Tallassee, Alabama. Cornelius and three of his children were working in a mill.

Neely Bowles — Neely Bowles enlisted as a private on January 28, 1862. No further records found.

V. Bowles — V. Bowles enlisted as a private on January 28, 1863. No further records found.

Walter Brannon — Walter Brannon enlisted as a private on May 12, 1862. He was captured at Marietta on June 18, 1864. He died at Martinsburg, Virginia.

James Henry Brawner — James Henry Brawner was born on July 3, 1825. He was the son of James M. and Mary Emma Blackmon Brawner. He married Lavonia David on January 5, 1858. Lavonia was the daughter of Jacob White David, an early pastor of Antioch Baptist Church in Harris County. James enlisted as a private on May 12, 1863. A year after he enlisted, he contracted a severe cold resulting in lung damage and hearing loss. He was discharged in 1863 due to his inability to perform his duties. After the war, the Brawners lived on River Road in Harris County. They owned more than 1,100 acres. Their family home still stands today. In 1890 James applied for a pension due to his disability. He was refused. He applied several more times. On October 29, 1903, James drank a small vial of carbolic acid. He died after several minutes in great agony. He was buried at Antioch Baptist Church in Harris County.

James Lemuel Brawner – James Lemuel Brawner enlisted as a private on November 5, 1862. The roll for February 28, 1863 shows him present. No further records found.

Mirabeau Lemuel Brawner — Mirabeau Lemuel Brawner was born in Harris County on July 17, 1839, the son of James and Emma Buchannan Brawner. He married Myra Walker on February 9, 1860. He enlisted as a sergeant on May 12, 1863. He surrendered at Greensboro, North Carolina on April 26, 1865. After the war, he lived and farmed in Harris County. Mirabeau and Myra had two sons and four daughters. In 1894, he married Annie Missouri Campbell and they had a son and daughter. Though he lived most of his life in the Blue Springs area of Harris County, he died on October 17, 1925 in LaGrange. Mirabeau was buried in the Mountain Hill Baptist Church Cemetery in Harris County.

S. Braynard — S. Braynard enlisted as a private on May 12, 1862. He was discharged at Savannah on July 18, 1864. No further records found.

Tomlinson Fort Brewster — Tomlinson Fort Brewster was born in Cherokee County on June 10, 1834. He was the son of Dr. John Brewster and Louisa Downs, both natives of South Carolina. After the death of his father, Dr. Brewster went to live with his uncle, Dr. B. D. Brewster, in Talbot County, with whom he began the study of medicine. In 1856 he graduated at the Jefferson medical college in Philadelphia, and in the same year he married Margaret Beal (December 11, 1856) and made his home, and the field of his early professional career, in Harris County.

According to Louise Calhoun Barfield in *The History of Harris County*, "Dr. Brewster was a large man with a big mustache and a very loud voice. When he drove into Cataula, he could be heard all over the village. He was a great singer." The advent of war found him there, busily engaged in medical work, and he promptly tendered his services to the Confederate government, volunteering as a private, and was elected first lieutenant of the unit. Dr. Brewster, during the last year of the war, was on duty as assistant surgeon in the hospital service at Columbus.

At the close of the war, he returned to his practice in Harris County and remained there until 1888, when he made his home in Atlanta. He became superintendent of Grady Memorial Hospital in Atlanta. He also served several terms in the state legislature. Dr. Brewster died on May 1, 1910 and was buried in Oakland Cemetery in Atlanta.

Isaac Brigman — Isaac Brigman enlisted as a private on November 7, 1862. The roll for February 29, 1864 shows him present. He was buried at Linwood Cemetery in Columbus.

Thomas Brigman — Thomas Brigman was born on May 19, 1824. He enlisted as a private on November 7, 1862. He was appointed Corporal on June 15, 1864. He was released from a hospital in Crawford, Alabama suffering from diarrhea and extreme debility. He took the oath of allegiance to the U.S. Government on December 31, 1864. He died on November 27, 1896. Thomas is buried in Girard Cemetery in Phenix City, Alabama.

J. Broadway — J. Broadway enlisted as a private on October 31, 1862. He was discharged at Beaulieu near Savannah on October 31, 1862. Broadway is buried in Linwood Cemetery in Columbus.

John M. Brown — John M. Brown enlisted as a private on January 18, 1863. He is shown on detail duty in the Engineer's Department December 22, 1863–February 29, 1864. No further records found.

John R. Brown — John R. Brown was born in 1816 in Tattnall County, Georgia. He enlisted as a private on May 20, 1862. According to pension records, he was on detail to build pontoon bridges till the close of the war. John was living in Emmanuel County in 1898. No further records found.

Benjamin F. Bryan — Benjamin F. Bryan was born in Muscogee County on July 5, 1845. He enlisted as a private on May 12, 1862. He was discharged with a disability in October 1863. He enlisted as a private in Co. F, 5th Reg. Georgia Reserve Infantry in May 1864. He was on detail to guard bridges in South Carolina March–April 1865. He married Mary Eugenia Slaton on September 16, 1870. They had two sons according to his pension records. Benjamin died on January 25, 1922 and was buried in Bethany Baptist Church Cemetery in Pine Mountain, Georgia (unmarked grave).

C. C. Buce — C. C. Buce enlisted as a private on February 11, 1862. He was on roll February 29, 1864. Buce was paroled at Montgomery, Alabama on May 18, 1865. No further records found.

E. Bullard — E. Bullard enlisted as a private on May 4, 1862. He deserted on May 20, 1862. No further records found.

Henry Cash — Henry Cash enlisted as a private on March 4, 1862. He was sick in camp on February 29, 1864. No further records found.

Jacob Taylor Chalker — Jacob Taylor Chalker was born on May 3, 1844, the son of Phillip and Jane Ann Landrum Chalker. He enlisted on March 2, 1863. His was wounded in his right arm at Kennesaw Mountain on June 18, 1864. According to his pension record, "He was shot through the right arm just below the elbow, the front bone came out, the arm shrank away and became crooked and has been this way ever since. This arm is essentially and substantially useless and that he is practically incompetent to perform the ordinary manual vocations of life." He married Macy Catherine Alcy Matthews on February 25, 1866. They had six sons and five daughters. After the war Jacob returned to farming in the area around Kennesaw, Georgia. Jacob died on April 12, 1906 and was buried in Kennesaw City Cemetery.

James Claxton — James Claxton enlisted on January 23, 1864. The roll for February 29, 1864 shows him present. No further records found.

James A. Cochran — James A. Cochran enlisted as a private on May 12, 1862. James transferred to Co. F on January 7, 1863. No further records found.

Columbus Collins — Columbus Collins enlisted as a private in Co. K, 46th Regiment on March 4, 1862. He was discharged (being underage) on August 6, 1862. He enlisted as a private in Co. H, 54th Regiment on January 28, 1863. He last appeared on roll January–February 1863. No further records found.

James Cook — James Cook enlisted as a private on January 28, 1863. No further records found.

S. S. Cook — S. S. Cook enlisted as a private on January 28, 1863. He surrendered at Greensboro, North Carolina on April 26, 1865. No further records found.

William W. Cook — William Cook enlisted as a private on January 28, 1863. He was wounded in his left shoulder and admitted to C.S.A. Hospital #11 in Charlotte, North Carolina on March 30, 1865. William was furloughed on April 14, 1865. No further records found.

Noah Corbitt — Noah Corbitt enlisted as a private on February 10, 1863. He was on roll February 29, 1864. No further records found.

Thomas Crutchfield — Thomas Crutchfield enlisted as a private on December 9, 1862. He was on roll February 29, 1864. No further records found.

Owen Cummings — Owen Cummings enlisted as a private on May 3, 1862. Owen transferred to Co. A on September 1, 1862. He died of pneumonia in Savannah in January 1863.

Thomas J. Doggett — Thomas Doggett enlisted as a private on March 15, 1863. He was on detail duty in the Engineer's Department December 22, 1863–February 29, 1864. No further records found.

Joseph T. Dorough — Joseph Dorough enlisted as a private on January 28, 1863. He was a detail nurse in the Bethesda, Georgia hospital in January 1864. He was reported present on the hospital roll of Joe Thompson Artillery on February 29, 1864. In 1867 he was listed in the Harris County Reconstruction Oath book. No further records found.

Luther Dowdell — Luther Dowdell was born on July 28, 1842 in Alabama, the son of James and Caroline Smith Dowdell. He enlisted as a private on July 18, 1863. He was elected 2nd Lieutenant later that year. He surrendered at Greensboro, North Carolina on April 26, 1865. After the war, he married Margaret L. Huguley on November 20, 1867 and settled in Auburn, Alabama. Luther and Margaret had six daughters and four sons. Luther farmed in the area until the turn of the century. He died on August 28, 1916 and was buried in the Little Texas Cemetery in Macon County, Alabama. After Luther's death, his wife applied for a pension in Macon County, Alabama.

George W. Dunaway — George W. Dunaway was born in Warren County on August 28, 1838. He enlisted as a private on February 24, 1864. Pension records show he was discharged at Savannah in December 1864.

Lew Curtis Dunaway — Lew Curtis Dunaway enlisted as a private on May 20, 1862. The roll for February 29, 1864, the last on file, shows him present. He was born in 1836 in Warren County. After the war he married Mary Rachel Alethia "Mollie" Wall on November 15, 1887.They had six sons and one daughter. In 1880, he is listed in the McDuffie County Agricultural Census. He died in 1900 and was buried at Mt. Horeb Baptist Church in Wrens, Georgia.

Thomas Dunaway — Thomas Dunaway enlisted as a private on May 20, 1862. He surrendered at Greensboro, North Carolina on April 26, 1865. No further records found.

William Dunaway — William Dunaway enlisted as a private on August 13, 1863. He surrendered at Greensboro, North Carolina on April 26, 1865. No further records found.

J. D. Dyal — J. D. Dyal enlisted as a private on May 12, 1862. He transferred to Co. K in 1862. He was discharged at Beaulieu near Savannah in September 12, 1862. No further records found.

Adoniriam Judson Ely — See page 148.

George Wilborn Ely — See page 148.

James D. Ely — See page 148.

Marcus B. Ely — See page 146–47.

Anderson Everidge — Anderson Everidge enlisted as a private on November 28, 1862. He appeared on roll February 29, 1864. No further records found.

____ Felzer — Felzer enlisted as a private on May 12, 1862. He was appointed Corporal. Felzer was discharged on October 31, 1862. No further records found.

Henry Freeman — Henry Freeman enlisted as a musician on May 10, 1862. He transferred to the Regimental Band January 29, 1863. No further records found.

Jasper Goodman — Jasper Goodman enlisted as a private on May 12, 1862. No further records found.

Joseph G. Goodman — Joseph Goodman was born in Mitchell County, Georgia on September 2, 1843. He enlisted as a private on January 27, 1863. He was captured at Atlanta on July 22, 1864. Goodman was transferred from Camp Chase, Ohio to City Point, Virginia for exchange on March 2, 1865. He was received at Boulware & Cox's Wharves in James River, Virginia March 10–12, 1865. In his pension records he stated he had a wife and eight children. Aaron Land wrote that Goodman had been captured at Kennesaw.

Charles Gorman — Charles Gorman enlisted as a musician on May 10, 1862. He transferred to the Regimental Band on January 29, 1863. No further records found.

James T. Hamer — James T. Hamer was born in Georgia on August 9, 1843. He enlisted as a 4th Corporal on May 12, 1862. He was wounded in his right eye, resulting in loss of sight, at Powder Springs, Georgia on June 18, 1864 during a picket engagement. James was in a hospital in Macon at the close of the war. James married Sarah ______ in 1867. They settled in Oneal's Mill in Troup County, Georgia, where James farmed. They had two sons and three daughters. James died on March 23, 1922 and is buried in the O'Neal Cemetery in Troup County.

William Hancock — William Hancock enlisted as a private on May 20, 1862. He was appointed Corporal. He surrendered at Greensboro, North Carolina on April 26, 1865. No further records found.

William J. Hart — William J. Hart was born March 11, 1837 in Harris County, the son of Solomon Hart and Elizabeth Mathews. He married Adeline Jones on January 3, 1860 in Harris County. William enlisted as a 4th Sergeant on May 12, 1862. He surrendered at Greensboro, North Carolina on April 26, 1865. In 1880, William and Adeline were living in Cataula, farming. They had five daughters and four sons. In 1900, he applied for a pension stating he was indigent. His farm of 100 acres had been sold five years before to pay debts. No further information could be found.

William H. Harvey — Harvey enlisted as a private on March 1, 1863. The roll for February 29, 1864, the last on file, shows him present.

Joseph Adkin Hewell — Joseph Hewell was born on December 2, 1826 in Wilkes County, Georgia, the son of Joseph Addison Hewell and Rebecca Lipscomb. On December 2, 1847 he married Harriet Cavey. They settled in Muscogee County, where Joseph farmed. They had a son and daughter. Harriet died sometime before 1850 and he married Aquila Dean. They had four daughters and four sons. He enlisted as a private on January 28, 1862. The roll for December 31, 1863 shows him present. On June 24, 1864, during the battle at Kennesaw Mountain, Joseph was wounded in the head, resulting in deafness and the loss of his left eye. After the war, Joseph continued to farm in Chattahoochee County, Georgia. Joseph died on November 24, 1899. He was buried in the Jamestown Cemetery in Chattahoochee County.

Seaborn Jones Hightower — Seaborn Jones Hightower was born on November 24, 1825 in Greene County, Georgia, the son of Seaborn Jones Hightower and Martha Holly. He married Georgia Tabitha Morgan in 1858. They had a son and daughter. He enlisted as a private on May 12, 1862. He was accidentally wounded in the left arm at Atlanta on July 9, 1864. His arm was amputated near the shoulder. He died at the Confederate Soldier's Home in Atlanta on August 29, 1910. He was buried in the Westview Cemetery in Atlanta.

William J. Hightower — William J. Hightower enlisted as a private on May 12, 1862. He was elected 2nd Lieutenant on July 5, 1862. He was dropped from the roll by General Beauregard on January 7, 1863. No further records found.

D. W. Holloway — D. W. Holloway enlisted as a private on February 26, 1863. He was paroled at Albany, Georgia on May 19, 1865. No further records found.

Levi Jefferson Horn — Levi Jefferson "Jeff" Horn was born in Harris County on August 6, 1847, the son of Thomas Horn and Sarah Blackman. He enlisted as a private in November 1862. He served as a private in Co. H, 54th Regiment for nine months and resigned. In 1864 he enlisted as a private in Co. G, 9th Regiment Georgia Militia. He was paroled in 1865. He married Saphrona ________ and they had a son and daughter. After the war, Jefferson farmed, living in Harris County. He died on July 4, 1930 and was buried in the Shady Grove Cemetery in Harris County.

Thomas Jefferson Horne — Thomas Jefferson Horne was born in Harris County in 1847. He enlisted as a private on November 5, 1862. Pension records show that he enlisted in Co. I, 9th Regiment, Georgia Militia in May 1864. He was paroled in 1865. No further records found.

Edwin A. Houston — Edwin A. Houston was born on October 13, 1844, the son of George and Nancy Houston. He enlisted as a private on January 28, 1863. The roll for February 24, 1864 shows him present. He married Martha Bird Fitzpatrick Dawkins on November 15, 1866. They had two sons and two daughters. Houston died on March 22, 1875 in Lee County, Alabama. He was buried in the Salem Cemetery in Salem, Alabama.

William Lafayette Howard — William Lafayette Howard enlisted as a private on January 28, 1863. He was killed in Atlanta on July 22, 1864.

Andrew Jackson Hubbard — Andrew Jackson Hubbard was born on August 5, 1835 in Henry County, the son of Peter Hubbard and Caroline Teale. He married Julia Ann Teal on May 10, 1853. They had one son. Andrew enlisted as a 2nd Corporal on May 12, 1862. His brothers, Erasmus and Richard, were also in the unit. He surrendered at Greensboro, North Carolina on April 26, 1865. After the war Andrew Hubbard lived in Harris County and worked as a farm laborer. By 1880 the family owned a farm in Harris County. According to the 1910 census, Andrew and Julia were living in rural Muscogee County. Andrew died on September 16, 1916 and was buried in the Getzen Memorial Baptist Church Cemetery. (Though unmarked, the church cemetery records show these two graves as Andrew and Richard Hubbard's.)

Erasmus Hubbard — Erasmus Hubbard was born in Georgia in 1853, the son of Peter Hubbard and Caroline Teale. He enlisted as a private on February 5, 1864. Though there are no written descriptions of his death in 1864, there is one statement about sending the deceased's belongings home, found in the Civil War records.

Richard Jackson Hubbard — Richard Jackson Hubbard was born on September 15, 1842, the son of Peter Hubbard and Caroline Teale. He enlisted as a private on January 27, 1863. The roll for February 29, 1864, the last on file, shows him present. Pension records stated that he was at home, sick on furlough, at the end of the war. Richard married Sandra Christian on February 11, 1869 in Harris County. They had three sons and four daughters. Richard farmed in Harris County for the next thirty years; he also sold produce from his farm. The 1900 census stated his occupation as a produce peddler. Richard died on July 23, 1929 in the community of Nances (Muscogee County). He is buried at Getzen Memorial Baptist Church Cemetery in Fortson, Georgia.

J. Cater Huckaby — J. Cater Huckaby enlisted as a private on May 12, 1862. He was captured at Jonesboro on August 31, 1864. He was exchanged at Rough and Ready, Georgia September 19–22, 1864. He died in Macon and is buried there in Rose Hill Cemetery.

Oliver B. Huckaby — Oliver B. Huckaby enlisted as a private on May 12, 1862. The roll for February 19, 1864 shows him present. No further records found.

Raymond R. Hutchison — Raymond R. Hutchinson was born in Warren County on October 27, 1817. He married Lucinda Langford on December 12, 1845 in Upson County, Georgia. He enlisted as a private on August 25, 1862. He surrendered at Greensboro, North Carolina on April 26, 1865. After the war, Hutchinson moved to Meriwether County and lived there until his death.

Seaborn L. Jones — Seaborn L. Jones was born on July 26, 1826. Jones enlisted and was appointed 2nd Corporal of Co. B, 1st Regiment Georgia Infantry (Ramsey's) on March 18, 1861. He mustered out at Augusta on March 18, 1862. He enlisted as a private in Co. H, 54th Regiment Georgia Infantry on August 13, 1863. The roll for February 29, 1864, the last on file, shows him present. After the war, Seaborn lived and farmed in Harris County until his death on July 31, 1904. He was buried in the Harmony Baptist Church Cemetery in Cataula. (The church no longer exists.)

C. B. Kendrick — C. B. Kendrick enlisted as a private in Co. C, 2nd Regiment, Georgia Infantry on October 21, 1861. He enlisted as a private in Co. H, 54th Regiment, Georgia Infantry on May 12, 1862. The roll for February 29, 1864, the last on file, shows him present.

William Kendrick — William Kendrick enlisted as a private on May 12, 1862. No further records found.

Henry A. J. Kennon — Henry A. J. Kennon was born in Upson County on February 5, 1837. He enlisted as a private on May 12, 1862. He surrendered at Greensboro, North Carolina on April 26, 1854. He married Lucinda _________. They had four sons and one daughter. After the war, Kennon performed carpentry work and farmed in Harris County. He died after 1908. No further records were found.

James A. Kilcrease — James A. Kilcrease enlisted as a private on January 28, 1863. He transferred to Co. F, 63rd Regiment Georgia Infantry on February 1, 1864. No further records found.

Aaron Land — Aaron Land was born in Coweta County, Georgia on February 24, 1834, the son of Jacob Land and Anna Herring. He married Angeline Polk Lokey on December 6, 1860. They had six sons and six daughters. Aaron and his brother John enlisted together on May 12, 1862. The following is an excerpt from Angeline Lokey Land's journal recounting Aaron's war experiences. (The following article was also printed in the *Columbus Ledger-Enquirer* on April 16, 1961.)

I enlisted in the Confederate Army about the First of May, 1862. I went out as an Orderly Sergeant of Company H, Fifty-Fourth Georgia Regiment [organized in Muscogee County]. Captain Charles Russell was in command of the Company, and Colonel Charlton H. Way in command of the Regiment. Our Regiment was in General Mercers Brigade. After serving a while on the coast at Savannah, I was elected Second Lieutenant of our Company H. Afterwards we was moved from the coast and joined the Tennessee Army, attached to Walker's Division. We were reorganized, and I was made First Lieutenant of our Company. (General Walker was killed at Atlanta. After the death of General Walker, we were under General Cleborn. General Cleborn was killed at Franklin, Tennessee, after which we were under General Cheatam, under whom we served until the Surrender.) After leaving the coast, we served a while in South Carolina and then joined the Tennessee Army above Dalton, Georgia. After fighting and falling back to Atlanta, we continued to Jonesboro, then back to Lovejoy Station, then to Palmetto Station, then back to Dalton, then to Decatur, Alabama, then to Tuscumbia, Ala., and then we crossed the Tennessee River and went to Franklin, Tennessee. We went as near to Nashville as we could get, and then to Murfreesboro, and then back to Franklin. We marched from Murfreesboro back to Franklin - a distance of seventy-five miles - in a day and night, and there my shoes gave out, so I wrapped my feet in pieces of blanket. We marched back to Tuscumbia, Ala., and from there to Vicksburg, Miss., thence to Lauderdale Springs, Miss. My feet was frostbitten and swollen so I couldn't travel, and I remained at Lauderdale Springs, at the hospital six weeks, and then came on through Meridian, Miss. I taken breakfast at Meridian. Then I came onto Columbus and stayed at home a few days. I then went to my command at Augusta, Ga. We proceeded to Columbia, South Carolina, and on to Raleigh, North Carolina, and finally to Smithfield, North Carolina. There we waited for orders. We were expecting to join the Virginia Army, but General Lee was surrounded by the enemy and had to surrender. Thus, we were disbanded at Smithfield.

After the war, the growing Land family settled down in rural Muscogee County. Aaron had a large farm, despite the economic conditions following the Civil War. Aaron was active in the Camp Benning Confederate Veteran's Association. He also served on the Muscogee County Board of Education. The Land family joined Mt. Moriah Primitive Baptist Church, where Aaron served as a deacon. On October 11, 1901 Aaron Land died from a heart attack. He was buried at Mt. Moriah Primitive Baptist Church Cemetery.

Harvey Monroe Land — Harvey Monroe Land was born on August 20, 1844 in Columbus, the son of Moses and Julia Huckaby Land. He enlisted as a private in the Co. H, 54th Regiment, Georgia Infantry in April 1863. He transferred to Co. B, 37th Georgia Infantry on September 15, 1863. On November 30, 1864 he was wounded in his leg at Franklin, Tennessee, and on December 25 he was captured at Pulaski, Tennessee. After a short hospitalization, he was transferred from Nashville, Tennessee to Louisville, Kentucky. He was later transferred to Camp Chase, Ohio and remained there until his release on June 13, 1865. He married Texana Victoria Campbell on March 23, 1867. They had three sons and three daughters. In 1880, the family was living in Tallapoosa County, Alabama, where Harvey worked as a farm laborer. After Texana died (1883), he married Martha Givings. They had a daughter and two sons. In 1900 the family was living in Cottonton, Alabama. They owned a farm in the area. His 1899 Alabama pension application stated that the wounds he received in the war rendered him unable to perform manual labor. Harvey died on June 4, 1902 and was buried in the Mt. Lebanon Baptist Church Cemetery in Cottonton, Alabama.

John Henry Land — John Henry Land was born on December 10, 1845, the son of Jacob and Anna Herring. He enlisted with his brother Aaron on May 1, 1862. He surrendered at Greensboro, North Carolina on April 26, 1865. John married Missouri Winifred Annah Lokey in Muscogee County on December 14, 1865. Between 1870 and 1900, the Land family moved to Cass, Texas and farmed. They had five sons and three daughters. In 1910, John was farming in Caddo, Louisiana with his wife. John died in October 1923 and is buried in the Vivian Cemetery in Vivian, Louisiana.

William Pierce Langford — William Pierce Langford was born in McDuffie County on June 6, 1846, the son of Thomas Langford and Martha Langston. He married Alice Green. They had five sons. He enlisted as a private on May 12, 1862. Langford surrendered at Greensboro, North Carolina on April 26, 1865. After the war, the Langford family settled in Harris County and farmed. Langford died in Pine Mountain on March 26, 1864. He was buried in the Bass Family Cemetery in Pine Mountain.

M. A. Marshall ("Babe") — Babe Marshall enlisted as a private on May 12, 1862. He surrendered at Greensboro, North Carolina on April 26, 1865. He died in Harris County on July 12, 1900. He is buried in the old Hopewell Methodist Church Cemetery (now abandoned and on private property) in Harris County.

John J. Massey — John J. Massey lived in the Mountain Hill area of Harris County. He married Sarah Ann Cook on October 15, 1846. Massey enlisted as a private on December 8, 1862. The roll for February 24, 1864, the last on file, shows him present.

William Albert McCants — William Albert McCants enlisted as a private on September 15, 1863. He was captured at Resaca on May 16, 1864. He died of typhoid malarial fever in the military prison at Louisville, Kentucky on May 31, 1864. He is buried in Cave Hill Cemetery in Louisville.

Clay M. McCoy — Clay M. McCoy enlisted as a 5th Sergeant on May 12, 1862. He surrendered at Thomasville, Georgia on May 23, 1865.

B. B. McCraw — B. B. McCraw enlisted as a private on May 12, 1862. He was absent without leave from February 26, 1863. No later records found.

William H. McGee — William H. McGee enlisted as a private on December 6, 1862. The roll for February 29, 1864, the last on file, shows him present. No further records found.

Valerius A. McGinty — Valerius A. McGinty enlisted as a private on September 3, 1862. He was captured at Salisbury, North Carolina on April 12, 1865. McGinty was released at Camp Chase, Ohio on June 13, 1865.

Abraham McLeroy — Abraham McLeroy was born in Harris County on November 27, 1836, the son of Needham McLeroy and Sara Herring. Abraham married Elizabeth Walker in Harris County on February 3, 1861. They had two sons and two daughters. Abraham enlisted as a private, along with his brother Nathan, on May 12, 1862. The roll for February 29, 1864, the last on file, shows him present. Pension records show he was severely wounded at New Hope Church, Georgia on June 5, 1864. He remained in the field hospital until July 15, 1864. He was sent to Columbus in August 1864, where he remained until April 26, 1865. After the war, the McLeroy family farmed in Harris County and later they moved to Columbus, where Abraham became a butcher. Abraham contracted typhoid fever and died on February 3, 1901. He was buried in the Richardson Cemetery in Harris County.

Nathan McLeroy — Nathan McLeroy was born in January 1834, the son of Needham McLeroy and Sara Herring. He married Nancy Jane Williams and they had three daughters and one son. He enlisted along with his brother Abraham as a private on May 12, 1862. The roll for February 29, 1864, the last on file, shows him present. By 1880, the McLeroys had moved to Clay County, Alabama and were farming. No further records were found.

John W. Miller — John W. Miller enlisted as a private on October 14, 1863. He was killed at Big Shanty, Georgia on June 9, 1864.

Allen Moody — Allen Moody enlisted as a private on May 12, 1862. He transferred to Co. K in 1862, then to Co. F on January 1, 1863. He was last on roll for February 28, 1863.

William B. Moore — William B. Moore enlisted as a private on September 1, 1862. He surrendered at Greensboro, North Carolina on April 26, 1865.

A. J. Morgan — A. J. Morgan was born in Warren County on May 3, 1845. He enlisted as a private in February 1863. Pension records show he surrendered at Greensboro, North Carolina on April 26, 1865.

James Nathan Morgan — James Nathan Morgan was born on December 8, 1833, the son of Henry J. Morgan and Harriet Longino Morgan. He married Margaret Jane Rodgers in Muscogee County on December 14, 1864. They had six sons and three daughters. He enlisted as a private on August 12, 1862. He was shot in the left hand by a musket ball, leaving his left hand permanently disabled at Kennesaw Mountain, Georgia on June 20, 1864. After the war the family lived in Smiths Cross Roads in Harris County and farmed. He died on November 17, 1905 and was buried at Union Baptist Church Cemetery in Whitesville, Georgia.

Robert J. Morgan — Robert J. Morgan was born in Harris County on January 1, 1836. He enlisted as a private on May 12, 1862. He was on detail as a teamster from June 3, 1863–February 29, 1864. Pension records show he contracted rheumatism in both legs in service and was totally deaf from exposure in service.

Jackson A. Mullins — Jackson A. Mullins enlisted as a private on October 9, 1863. The roll for February 29, 1864 shows him present.

Henry L. Narramore — Henry L. Narramore enlisted as a private on April 11, 1863. He was furloughed for ten days on February 21, 1864. No later records.

Amos P. Norris — Amos P. Norris was born on May 3, 1845 in Warren County. He married Elizabeth Raley. They had five sons and three daughters. He enlisted as a private on February 24, 1864. Pension records show he surrendered at Greensboro, North Carolina on April 26, 1865. After the war, the family moved to Lincoln County, Georgia and farmed. Norris died in Columbia County, Georgia on February 16, 1911.

He was buried in the Marvin United Methodist Church Cemetery in Martinez, Georgia.

James Marcus Norris — James Marcus Norris was born in Warren County on March 18, 1844. He enlisted as a private on December 6, 1862 and surrendered at Greensboro, North Carolina on April 26, 1865.

L. B. Nunnally — L. B. Nunnally enlisted as a private on November 3, 1862. He took the oath of allegiance to the U.S. Government at Nashville, Tennessee on December 28, 1864.

Frank O'Conner — Frank O'Conner enlisted as a private on March 13, 1863. The roll for February 29, 1864, the last on file, shows him present.

Thomas H. Palmer — Thomas H. Palmer enlisted as a private on June 5, 1863. He was captured at Marietta on June 18, 1864. Palmer was paroled at Camp Morton, Indiana and forwarded to Point Lookout, Maryland for exchange on February 19, 1865.

W. J. Palmer — W. J. Palmer enlisted as a private on February 11, 1863. The roll for February 24, 1864, the last on file, shows him present. Palmer is buried in the Moon David Cemetery in Columbus.

James M. Perdue — James M. Perdue was born in Chattahoochee County in 1844. The roll for February 29, 1864, the last on file, shows him present. After the war Perdue farmed and worked as a carpenter. In 1895 he fell from a church roof, which resulted in complete paralysis.

William P. Phillips — William P. Phillips was born in Muscogee County. He enlisted as a private on March 23, 1863. He surrendered at Greensboro, North Carolina on April 26, 1865. According to his pension records, he was a farm laborer after the war until he could no longer work due to health issues. No further records found.

George Tillman Pigg — George Tillman Pigg was born in Chesterfield District, South Carolina in October 1820, the son of Johnny and Catherine Pigg. The family moved to Harris County around 1850. He enlisted as a substitute for R. F. Beal on January 16, 1863. The roll for February 29, 1864, the last on file, shows him present. After the war George Pigg worked as a farm laborer. The family later moved to Cullman, Alabama. He died in 1910 and is buried at Blair Methodist Church in Cullman.

C. L. Raiford — C. L. Raiford enlisted as a private on November 3, 1862. He surrendered at Greensboro, North Carolina on April 26, 1865. No further records found.

Jefferson Raley — Jefferson Raley enlisted as a private on May 12, 1862. The roll for February 29, 1864, the last on file, shows him present. No further records found.

John F. Raley — John F. Raley enlisted as a private on May 12, 1862. The roll for February 29, 1864, the last on file, shows him present. No further records found.

John Ramsey — John Ramsey enlisted as a private on September 1, 1862. He surrendered at Greensboro, North Carolina on April 26, 1865. No further records found.

W. A. Robinson — W. A. Robinson was appointed 3rd Sergeant of Captain Witt's Company (Express Infantry) on August 1, 1863. He transferred to Co. H, 54th Regiment Georgia Infantry on October 5, 1863. The roll for February 29, 1864, the last on file, shows him present. No further records found.

Adam Crall Rodgers — Adam Crall Rodgers was born in South Carolina on July 25, 1835, the son of Adam and Nancy Lathan Rodgers.

He enlisted as a private along with his brothers (James, Samuel, and William) on May 12, 1862. He surrendered at Greensboro, North Carolina on April 26, 1865. Adam married Julia Frances Murrah in 1872. They had two daughters. The Rodgerses lived in Harris County and owned a farm. Adam died in April 1920. He is buried in the Nelson Cemetery in Harris County.

James McCurdy Rodgers — James McCurdy Rodgers was born in South Carolina on October 29, 1829, the son of Adam and Nancy Lathan Rodgers. He married Carolyn Amelia Pool in 1851. They had four daughters and one son. He enlisted as a private along with his brothers (Adam, Samuel, and William) on May 12, 1862. He was sick in the Bethesda hospital from January 16–February 29, 1864. No later records were found. After the war the Rodgerses farmed in Muscogee County. James was a member of Camp Benning Confederate Veteran's Association. James Rodgers died on September 9, 1908 in Muscogee County. He is buried in the Mt. Moriah Baptist Church Cemetery in Columbus.

Robert Rodgers — Robert Rodgers enlisted as a private on January 21, 1864. The roll for February 29, 1864, the last on file, shows him present. No further records found.

Samuel Craig Rodgers — Samuel Craig Rodgers was born in York, South Carolina on August 9, 1836, the son of Adam and Nancy Lathan Rodgers. He married Susan Winifred Pool on October 12, 1858. They had five sons and four daughters. He enlisted as a private along with his brothers (Adam, James, and William) on May 12, 1862. The roll for February 1864, the last on file, shows him present. Pension records show he surrendered at Greensboro, North Carolina on April 26, 1865. After the war the Rodgers family farmed in Muscogee County. Samuel Rodgers died in Columbus on January 15, 1915. He is buried in the Mt. Moriah Primitive Baptist Church cemetery in Muscogee County.

T. J. Rodgers — T. J. Rodgers enlisted as a private on November 12, 1862. He was discharged by civil authority on January 20, 1864. No further records found. He is buried at Camp Hill Cemetery, Camp Hill, AL.

William Matthew Rodgers — William Matthew Rodgers was born in South Carolina on November 26, 1838, the son of Adam and Nancy Lathan Rodgers. He married Frances Elizabeth Champion on January 22, 1861 in Muscogee County. They had three sons and four daughters. Matthew enlisted as a 1st Corporal on May 12, 1862, along with his brothers (Adam, James, and Samuel). The roll for February 29, 1864, the last on file, shows him present. Pension records show he surrendered at Greensboro, North Carolina on April 26, 1865. After the war the Rodgers family farmed in Harris County. William Rodgers died in Birmingham, Alabama on February 11, 1918. He is buried in the Cedarwood Cemetery in Roanoke, Alabama.

Charles Rienzi Russell — Charles Rienzi Russell was born in Muscogee County on May 15, 1837, the son of William R. and Mary Russell. When his father died, Osborn Ely became his guardian. Charles attended the University of Georgia and received an appointment in the Treasury Department in Washington, D.C. He resigned his Treasury Department post in early 1861 and enlisted as a private in Co. G, 2nd Regiment, Georgia Infantry on April 16, 1861. He was elected 2nd Lieutenant of Co. C on July 24, 1861, then 1st Lieutenant on April 28, 1862. He resigned in May 1862 after the Virginia Campaign and organized his own company, the Russell Guards (Co. H, 54th Reg., Ga. Vol. Inf.), on May 12, 1862. Colonel Charles H. Olmstead, in his memoirs, recounted an amusing story about Capt. Russell:

I spoke of the passage of the Flint as having been made without difficulty and so it was for all excepting for Captain Charlie Russell of the 54th. As the regiment got to the bank and looked at the yellow water of unknown depth, the men hesitated a little before entering the stream-noticing this, Russell, who was always inclined to be melodramatic, waved his sword and shouted "Don't be afraid of a little water men; it's only knee deep. Follow me!" Then he stepped in up to his neck, having unfortunately found a place where the current had washed a hole under the bank. Of course there was a great shout of laughter as the men went on either side of him through the shallow water.

His obituary stated that he fought under Pat Cleburne in Tennessee and was with Johnston and Hood in all the fighting back to Atlanta. He was in the thickest fighting at Peachtree Creek. At Little Kennesaw a shell killed a member of his company right next to him and knocked him unconscious. The concussion of the shell damaged his hearing, which grew progressively worse throughout the rest of his life. He surrendered at Greensboro, North Carolina on April 26, 1865. He married Anna Robison on July 19, 1866 in Columbus. They settled in Columbus, where Russell practiced law. They had one son and three daughters. Charles Russell died on April 7, 1891 and is buried in Linwood Cemetery in Columbus.

D. G. Russell — D. G. Russell enlisted as a private on May 12, 1862. He was on detail duty, clerk to Adjutant, on February 29, 1864. No later records found.

Rollen A. Russell — Rolin A. Russell was born in Muscogee County in 1844, the son of William and Mary Russell and the brother of Charles Russell. He enlisted as a Jr. 2nd Lieutenant in the Russell Guards on May 12, 1862. He resigned from the Russell Guards and was elected Lieutenant of Co. F, 64th Regiment, Georgia Infantry on May 11, 1863. Russell was wounded through the right hip, which left him partly paralyzed. He was captured at Deep Bottom, Virginia on August 16, 1864. Rollen was released at Fort Delaware on June 17, 1865. After the war, he lived with his sister, Carrie Greer, and practiced law in Harris and Muscogee County. He married Mollie Lowe in Harris County on March 11, 1891. Russell died in Hamilton on March 24,

1908. He is thought to be buried in the Hamilton City Cemetery in Harris County in an unmarked grave.

David Sallas — David Sallas was born on September 27, 1821 in Georgia. He married Louisa McIntosh on November 27, 1845 in Russell County, Alabama. They had three sons and three daughters. In 1860 he was living in Russell County and owned a farm. Sallas enlisted as a private on October 3, 1863. He was mortally wounded near Atlanta on July 4, 1864. He is buried in the Mt. Lebanon Church Cemetery in Cottonton, Alabama.

Ephraim G. Sallas — Ephraim G. Sallas, the brother of David Sallas, was born in Georgia in 1827. He married Sarah E. Moore. The family settled in Russell County, Alabama. They had three sons and seven daughters. Ephraim, the brother of David Sallas, enlisted as a private on November 2, 1863. He was later appointed Corporal. He surrendered at Greensboro, North Carolina on April 26, 1865. After the war, the Sallas family continued to farm in Russell County, Alabama. He died on July 25, 1900 and is buried in the Oswichee Baptist Church Cemetery in Russell County, Alabama.

W. W. Shanks — W. W. Shanks enlisted as a private on May 12, 1862. He deserted on May 14, 1862. No further records found.

A. Silas — A. Silas enlisted as a private on September 4, 1862. He deserted at Savannah on June 23, 1863. No further records found.

G. W. Spear — G. W. Spear enlisted as a private on November 12, 1862. He deserted on March 18, 1863. He was admitted to U.S.A. General Hospital Ladies' Home in New York City on April 18, 1863. He returned to duty in April 1863 and was paroled on April 20, 1863. He was admitted to U.S.A. Convalescent Hospital at Fort Wood, Bedloe Island in New York on April 20, 1863. He transferred to the 51st Hospital on April 21, 1863. No later records found.

James Samuel Spear — James Samuel Spear enlisted as a private on May 12, 1862. He transferred to Co. F on January 1, 1863. Spear was captured at Kennesaw Mountain on June 18, 1864. He was released at Camp Morton, Indiana on May 22, 1865. He arrived back in Sasser, Georgia on May 31, 1865. Spear kept a day diary of his war experiences (now owned by a descendant). After the war, James S. Spear owned a sawmill in Sasser. He is buried in the Macedonia Baptist Church Cemetery in Sasser.

Calvin T. Spinks — Calvin T. Spinks was born April 15, 1829. He enlisted as a private in 1864 and was wounded and disabled at Jonesboro on September 1, 1864. Calvin Spinks died on March 11, 1901. He is buried at Union Baptist Church in Harris County.

Joseph F. Stevenson — Joseph F. Stephenson enlisted as a private on July 18, 1862. He was on detail as a nurse and nurse steward from October until December 1862. No later records found.

Abdiel Stott — Abdiel Stott was born on February 6, 1837 in Anderson, Alabama. He enlisted as a private in Co. E, 15th Battalion Alabama Partisan Rangers on May 8, 1862. He transferred to Co. H, 54th Regiment Georgia Infantry on September 14, 1862. The roll dated February 29, 1864, the last on file, shows him present. Abdiel Stott died on May 19, 1866 and is buried in the Stott Family Cemetery in Butler County, Alabama.

William B. Strawbridge — William B. Strawbridge was born in South Carolina in 1824. He married Jane A. Jackson in Talbot County on December 23, 1849. He was appointed postmaster in Ellerslie (Harris County) on September 12, 1855. He listed his occupation as a grocery merchant in the Harris County 1860 census. He enlisted as a private on November 3, 1862. He was appointed Ordnance Sergeant in December

1863. The roll for February 29, 1864, the last on file, shows him present. No further records found.

George M. Stribling — George M. Stribling enlisted as a private on November 17, 1862. He surrendered at Greensboro, North Carolina on April 26, 1865. No further records found.

John A. Stribling — John A. Stribling enlisted as a private on May 12, 1862. The roll for February 29, 1864, the last on file, shows him present. John Stribling married Amada Attaway in Harris County on March 19, 1857. In 1860, the Striblings were living in the Mulberry Grove area of Harris County.

Milton Stribling — Milton Stribling enlisted as a private on May 12, 1862. He died on December 20, 1862. No further records found.

Ben A. Stripling— Ben A. Stripling was born in Harris County on February 17, 1842. He enlisted as a private on October 1, 1863. He was wounded in his knee and right eye near Decatur on August 9, 1864. He was given a discharge due to disability on October 9, 1864. Stripling married Amelia Jane Gullatte on November 16, 1866 in Harris County. They had three sons and five daughters. By 1880, the family had moved to Lee County, Alabama; the census stated that Stripling was a farmer. By 1890, the Striplings were living in Columbus and Ben applied for a pension due to disability. He died in Columbus on November 14, 1902. He was buried in the Chipley Cemetery in Pine Mountain.

Solomon T. Tarvin — Solomon T. Tarvin was born in Georgia on February 14, 1827. He married California McDonald in Harris County on January 26, 1854. They had two daughters. After the war the Tarvins farmed in Harris County. He enlisted as a private on November 3, 1862. He was in Lee Hospital at Columbus on October 31, 1864. No later records found. After the war the Tarvins farmed in Harris County.

Solomon Tarvin died in Columbus on January 10, 1904. He is buried in the Ellerslie United Methodist Church Cemetery in Harris County.

William Tarvin — William Tarvin was born in Columbia County on March 3, 1825. He married Ariada Ann Slaghter on December 23, 1851. They had five sons and four daughters. He enlisted as a private on November 3, 1863. The roll for February 29, 1864, the last on file, shows him present. He surrendered at Greensboro, North Carolina on April 26, 1865. After the war, the Tarvins settled in Harris County and farmed. William Tarvin died on December 29, 1911 and was buried in Riverdale Cemetery in Columbus.

Alexander Teel — Alexander Teel was born on April 1, 1838 in Harris County. He married Margaret Huey on April 26, 1860. Teel enlisted as a 2nd Sergeant on May 12, 1862. The roll for February 29, 1864, the last on file, shows him present. Alexander Teel died in Columbus on December 22, 1895.

Lafayette Thomas — Lafayette Thomas enlisted as a private in Co. B, 31st Regiment, Georgia Infantry on October 5, 1861. He was discharged for disability in 1862. He enlisted as a private in Co. H, 54th Regiment, Georgia Infantry on November 8, 1862. He transferred to Co. F, January 1, 1862. He was paroled at Thomasville on May 25, 1865.

William H. Thomas — William H. Thomas enlisted as a private on December 8, 1862. The roll for February 29, 1864, the last on file, shows him present. No further records found.

Henry Twilly — Henry Twilly was born in Alabama on October 7, 1845. He enlisted as a private on January 28, 1863. He was wounded in the right arm, necessitating amputation above the elbow, at Atlanta on July 22, 1864. He married Sarah Frances McCann in Muscogee County on August 30, 1871. They had two daughters. He worked as an overseer of a chain gang. In 1879, his former captain, Charles R. Russell, wrote that Henry "lost an arm while gallantly charging the enemies fortification on the day and year above mentioned." He was awarded $60 for loss of his arm. He died in 1900 in Columbus.

James P. Upton — James P. Upton enlisted as a private on January 28, 1863. The roll for

February 29, 1864, the last on file, shows him present. No further records found.

Franklin Veatch — Franklin Veatch was born as a private on March 1, 1863. He took the oath of allegiance to the U.S. Government at Nashville, Tennessee on December 30, 1864.

Nathaniel Wade — Nathaniel Wade enlisted as a private on September 10, 1862. The roll for February 29, 1864, the last on file, shows him present, on picket duty. No later records were found.

John J. Walker — John "Jack" Walker was born in Muscogee County, Georgia on March 12, 1846. He was appointed 3rd Corporal on May 12, 1862. He appears last on roll for February 28, 1863. Pension records show he enlisted as a private in Co. F, 5th Regiment, Georgia Reserve Infantry in 1864. He surrendered at Smithfield, North Carolina on April 26, 1865. After the war, he worked on a farm in the Columbus area. At the end of his life he was suffering from chronic arthritis and blindness. He died in Columbus in 1919.

James T. Weldon — James T. Weldon enlisted as a private on May 12, 1862. He transferred to Co. F. The roll for December 31, 1863, the last on file, shows him present.

William F. Whitehead — William F. Whitehead enlisted as a private on May 12, 1862. The roll for February 29, 1864, the last on file, shows him present, on picket duty. No later record.

George Washington Williams — George Washington Williams was born in North Carolina in 1862. He enlisted as a private on November 5, 1862. He was detailed to the Pioneer Corps in February 1864. They surrendered at Tallahassee, Florida on May 10, 1865. He was paroled at Thomasville on May 18, 1865. He died in 1910.

People and Places

Beaulieu — Camp Beaulieu was located on the Vernon River about 12 miles south of Savannah. The camp was situated across from the island of RoseDhu (Rose Dew). Part of the 54th Regiment located there in August 1862.

General P. T. Beauregard — The first Brigadier General in the Confederate States of America. He commanded the forces in the Charleston and Savannah areas in 1862 and 1863.

Joseph Brown — Served as governor of Georgia from 1857–1865, later serving as a senator (1880–1891).

Thomas A. Burke — Appointed Captain and Assistant Quartermaster of the 54th Regiment on April 30, 1862. By the end of the war, he was serving at Charleston, South Carolina as Major and Assistant Quartermaster. No further records found.

Chattahoochee River — A 430-mile-long river that starts in Northeast Georgia and travels southwesterly through Atlanta to the Georgia-Alabama River until it meets the Apalachicola River in Florida.

John G. Clarke — Appointed Commissary on April 30, 1862, then Captain and Assistant Quartermaster of the 54th Infantry on August 19, 1863. He served in that capacity until July 20, 1864. No later records found.

Mary Ely — Mary Ely was a slave belonging to the Ely family. Her Civil War records are attached to Marcus Ely. The letters mention Mary numerous times. She is listed in the compiled service records of Confederate soldiers. Late in 1864, Mary arrived in Savannah. She was hired to be a cook in the hospital under the supervision of Dr. J. H. Houston, Captain Hanleiter's Company, Georgia Light Artillery, Jo Thompson Artillery. The record states that she was hired by the consent of owner, to be paid $25 per month, and was the property of Lieutenant Ely.

Etowah River — A 164-mile-long river that starts in Dahlonega, Georgia and runs toward Rome, Georgia, where it flows into the Oostanaula River.

Dr. James Erwin Godfrey, Jr. — Born in 1835 in South Carolina. His father, James Erwin Godfrey, Sr., was appointed Chaplain of the 54th Regiment in 1862. James was appointed Surgeon of the Confederate States of America on April 27, 1861. He transferred to the 54th Regiment as Surgeon on May 10, 1862. Dr. Godfrey amputated James Ely's leg in Atlanta on July 22, 1862. After the war, he returned to Madison. He ran a grocery store and practiced medicine. He died in Madison on October 23, 1887.

Thomas J. Graves — Thomas Graves was a private in the 14th Battalion, Georgia Light Artillery, Montgomery's Division. He was a friend of Jerry Dumas and took care of him until his death. He wrote Mattie informing her of Jerry's illness and later his death.

Captain C. R. Hanleiter — Cornelius Redding Hanleiter was born in Savannah in 1815. He was orphaned at the age of eight and several years later apprenticed to William Robertson, a printer and publisher of the *Savanah Georgian*. At the age of 19, Hanleiter finished his apprenticeship and moved to Augusta to begin working in publishing. Hanleiter moved around the state working as a printer and publisher of various newspapers and journals. Although he opposed secession, with the coming of the Civil War, he served as lieutenant in several Georgia units. His primary duties involved constructing defensive installations around the city of Savannah. At the end of the war, he had risen to the rank of Colonel. As a result of the war, Hanleiter was financially ruined. Although he attempted to reestablish himself, he never attained the success he had experienced before the war. His most significant contributions included publication of the Atlanta City Directories from 1870, 1871, and 1872. For a brief time, he worked in Washington, D.C. in the Government Printing Office as a proofreader. Hanleiter died at the home of his daughter in April 1897. (This information was published in the *Atlanta Constitution* in April 1897 and on findagrave.com.)

Hardeeville, South Carolina — Located on the Savannah River, Hardeeville was the scene of several skirmishes due to the railway.

Dr. Joseph Hazel — A physician and friend of Marcus Ely. He lived in Beaufort, South Carolina and is buried in the cemetery of Cave Methodist Church. In 2008, a tornado destroyed the church and damaged the cemetery.

Dr. James Houston — James H. Houston was an assistant surgeon in the 38th Georgia Infantry, later changed to Joe Thompson Light Artillery. He served at Bethesda Hospital in Bethesda, Georgia.

Lovejoy Station — A small town near Atlanta involved in three battles during summer 1864.

Major William H. Mann — Elected Captain of Co. A, 1st Regiment, Georgia State Troops on October 3, 1861. He was elected Major of the 54th Reg., Georgia Infantry on May 16, 1862. He was killed in the Battle of Atlanta on July 22, 1864. His brother, Dr. John Mann, was killed a few days later in the same battle. They are both buried in the Greenwood Cemetery in Atlanta.

Thomas McLeroy — McLeroy didn't serve in the Civil War; he was already in his 60s. In the letters he was Uncle Tom McLeroy, the shoemaker. He was born in Clarke County in 1795. He married Martha Curosa Meadown in Oglethorpe County on February 10, 1824. They had two sons and two daughters. By 1860, they were living in Harris County. Thomas worked as a cobbler and ran a farm.

General Hugh Mercer — Mercer commanded a post of Savannah for most of the war. He joined General William Hardee during the Atlanta Campaign. After the war, he returned to Savannah and resumed his work in banking. He moved to Baltimore in 1869, where he worked as a commission merchant. He died in 1877 and is buried in Bonaventure Cemetery in Thunderbolt.

Montgomery — Montgomery was a summer retreat for wealthy Savannahians, located below Savannah on the Vernon River.

Oostanaula River — The Oostanaula begins in Gordon County and flows into the Coosa River that runs into Alabama.

Purrysburg, South Carolina — Purrysburg, on the Savannah River, was a colonial town settled in the early 1700s by Jean-Pierre dePury. Most of the settlers were Swiss Protestants. The town was later abandoned; the cemetery remains.

Lieutenant G. E. Thomas — G. E. Thomas later became a captain; he served in both F and G Companies in the 54th Georgia Regiment.

Tunnel Hill — Tunnel Hill, located in northwest Georgia, best known for the 1862 Great Locomotive Chase, was used as a base for planning by the Union during the Civil War. Sherman used the Clisby Austin House in Tunnel Hill as his planning headquarters for the Atlanta Campaign.

Jimmy and Kelon Watson — Jimmy and Kelon were the sons of Elizabeth and William Watson of Barnesville. Elizabeth Dumas Watson was Mattie Ely's sister. Jimmy and Kelon enlisted in the 32nd Georgia Infantry. They were involved in the Battle of Olustee near Jacksonville. Kelon was severely injured and later died in Charleston. No further records could be found on Jimmy Watson.

Colonel Charlton H. Way — Charlton Way was born in Liberty County on October 5, 1834, the son of William and Elizabeth Hanford Way. He attended the Georgia Military Institute in Marietta. Before the war, he worked as a commission merchant in Savannah. Way was elected Captain of his independent Co., Georgia Infantry (Forrest City Rangers) on July 18, 1861. He mustered out on November 1, 1861. He was elected Colonel of the 54th Regiment, Georgia Volunteer Infantry on May 16, 1862. He was in command of the 54th Regiment at the surrender in Greensboro, North Carolina on April 26, 1865. After the war, he became a cotton broker and real estate developer in Savannah. He died July 1, 1901 and is buried in North Laurel Grove Cemetery in Savannah.

White Bluff — A series of communities located about ten miles south of Savannah that included Nicholsonboro, Rose Dew, Twin Hill, and Cedar Grove.

Bibliography

1830 U.S. Federal Census
1840 U.S. Federal Census
1850 U.S. Federal Census
1860 U.S. Federal Census
1870 U.S. Federal Census
1880 U.S. Federal. Census
1900 U.S. Federal Census
1910 U.S. Federal Census
1920 U.S. Federal Census
"Abraham McLeroy Died on Thursday," *Columbus* (GA) *Daily Enquirer*, 30 June 1911, 2.
"The Attack on Charleston," *Connecticut Courant*, 18 April 1863, 1.
"Attack on Fort McAllister," *Daily Constitutionalist* (Augusta GA), 4 March 1863, 3.
Barfield, Louise Calhoun. *History of Harris County, GA, 1827–1961*. LaGrange GA: Cherith Creek Designs, 1991.
"Battle in Florida," *Macon* (GA) *Telegraph*, 24 February 1864, 2.
Boatner, Mark Mayo. *The Civil War Dictionary*. New York NY: Vintage Books, 1991.
"Brewster's Funeral Monday Afternoon," *The Atlanta Georgian*, 2 May 1910, 20.
Civil War Commission. *Crossroads of Conflict: A Guide to Civil War Sites in Georgia*. Athens GA: University of Georgia Press, 2010.
Coleman, Kenneth, editor. *A History of Georgia*. Athens GA: University of Georgia Press, 1982.
"Colonel Geo Ely Veterans Railroader a Popular Passenger Agent Who Is Well Known in Columbus," *Columbus* (GA) *Daily Enquirer*, 16 November 1909, 5.
"Company Wanted," *Daily Columbus* (GA) *Enquirer*, 29 April 1862, 2.
"Death Claims Dr. Brewster," *The Atlanta* (GA) *Constitution*, 2 May 1910, 20.
"Death of General T.R.R. Cobb," *Daily Constutionalist* (Augusta GA), 14 December 1862, 3.
"Death of Mr. Ed Ely," *Columbus* (GA) *Daily Enquirer*, 20 July 1881, 4.
"Death of Professor M.B. Ely," *Daily Enquirer Sun* (Columbus GA), 6 April 1880, 4.
"Departure of the French Consul at Charleston," *Macon* (GA) *Telegraph*, 4 April 1863, 1.

Evans, Tad. *Georgia Newspaper Clippings, Houston Co. Extracts, Vol. 1.* Savannah GA: Genealogy Publishers, 2005.

Famighetti, Robert, *1998 World Almanac and Book of Facts,* New York NY: St. Martin's Press, 1997.

"The Front – Heavy Battle at Resaca," *Macon* (GA) *Telegraph*, 17 May 1864, 1.

Gallman, J. Matthew. *The Civil War Chronicle, The Only Day-by-Day Portrait.* Old Saybrook CT: Ancourt Press, 2000.

"George W. Ely, Veteran Railroad Man Is Dead." *Montgomery Advertiser, Confederate Pension Applications.* Montgomery AL: Georgia Confederate Pension Office, RG 58-1-1, Georgia Archives.

Groves, Robert Walker. "Beaulieu Plantation." *The Georgia Historical Quarterly* 37/3 (September 1953): 200–209.

Guralnik, David B. *Webster's New World Dictionary of the American Language.* New York NY: The World Publishers Co, 1970.

Hawes, Lilla Mills, editor. *The Memoirs of Charles H. Olmstead.* Savannah GA: The Georgia Historical Society, 1964.

Henderson, Lillian. *Roster of the Confederate Soldiers of GA 1861–1865.* 6 Volumes. Hapeville GA: Longino and Pottery, Inc., 1960.

Hickey, Louise McHenry. *Rambling through Morgan County, GA.* Madison GA: Morgan County Historical Society, 1971; Reprint 1976.

http://www.answers.com/topic/millet

http://cdm.georgiaarchives.org:2011/cdm/singleitem/collection/vg2/id/3702/rec/2

http://www.civilwar.org/education/history/glossary/glossary.htnl#C

http://dictionary.reference.com/browse/foolscap

http://www.georgiaencyclopedia.org/history-archaeology/fortpulaski

http://www.findagrave.com

http://mckechnies.net/family/-references/medical.htm

http://www.morgancountyheritage.org/communities/godfrey/document/dr-je-godfrey

http://www.rootsweb.ancestry.com/~mnwabcw/31.htm

http://files.usgwarchives.net/ga/muscogee/bios/land.txt

"J.H. Brawner Ends His Life," *Columbus* (GA) *Daily Enquirer*, 31 October 1903, 8.

Jones, Charles Edgeworth. *Georgia in the Civil War 1861–1865.* Atlanta GA: Foote and Dunn, 1907.

Jones, Terry L. *The Historical Dictionary of the Civil War.* 2 Volumes. New York NY: Scarecrow Press, 2002.

Joslyn, Muriel Phillips. *Charlotte's Boys Civil War Letters of the Branch Family of Savannah.* Berryville VA: Rockbridge Publishing Co., 1996.

"Land Ancestor Tells Tales of 75-Mile Hike in 24 Hours," *Columbus* (GA) *Ledger-Enquirer Civil War Centennial Edition*, 16 April 1964.

Lattimore, Ralston B. *Fort Pulaski National Monument Georgia.* Washington DC: National Park Service Historical Handbook Series, 1954; Reprint 1961.

Martin, John H. *Columbus, Georgia from Its Selection as a "Trading Town" in 1827 to Its Partial Destruction by Wilson's Raid in 1865, Parts 1 & 2.* Columbus GA: Georgia Genealogical, 1874; Reprint 1972.

McCall, Ettie Tidwell. *Roster of Revolutionary Soldiers in Georgia.* 5 Volumes. Baltimore MD: Genealogical Publishing Co., 1969.

Miles, Jim. *Georgia Civil War Sites.* Warner Robins GA: J&R Graphics, 1987.

"Mr. Aaron Land Dies Suddenly," *Columbus* (GA) *Enquirer-Sun*, 12 October 1901, 5.

"The Murfreesboro Affair," *Macon* (GA) *Telegraph*, 25 July 1862, 1.

"Nashville Destroyed by the Enemy," *Macon* (GA) *Telegraph*, 3 March 1893, 3.

Nelson, Harold W., and Jay Luvaas. *Guide to the Atlanta Campaign: Rocky Face Ridge to Kennesaw Mountain.* Lawrence KS: University Press of Kansas, 2008.

"An Old Citizen of County Dead, James M. Rodgers," *Columbus* (GA) *Daily Enquirer*, 11 September 1908, 5.

opionator.blogs.nytimes.com/2013/12/26 the-salt-wars/

Ouchey, Kelby. *Flora and Fauna of the Civil War: An Environmental Reference Guide.* Baton Rouge LA: Louisiana State University Press, 2010.

Overby, Mary McKewon. *Obituaries Published in the Christian Index, 1822–1879.* Macon GA: Georgia Baptist Historical Society, Mercer University Press, 1975.

———. *Obituaries Published in the Christian Index, 1880–1899.* Macon GA: Georgia Baptist Historical Society Depository, Mercer University Press, 1982.

Russell County Historical Commission. *History of Russell Co., Alabama.* Dallas TX: National Sharp Graphics, 1982.

Schroeder-Lein, Glenna. *The Encyclopedia of Civil War Medicine.* Armonk NY: M.E. Sharpe, Inc., 2008.

Secrist, Philip. *Battle of Resaca: Atlanta Campaign, 1864.* Macon GA: Mercer University Press, 2010.

Sholes, A. E., publisher. *Sholes Directory of the City of Columbus.* Columbus GA: Thomas Gilbert Printer and Binder, 1878.

Simmons, Henry E. *A Concise Encyclopedia of the Civil War.* New York NY: A.S. Barnes and Co., 1965.

Smedlund, William S. *Campfires of Georgia Troops, 1861–1865.* Kennesaw GA: Kennesaw Mountain Press, 1995.

Telfair, Nancy. *A History of Columbus, GA, 1828-1928,* Columbus GA: Columbus Publishing Co., 1929.

"Terrible Slaughter on Board the Keokuk," *Daily Constitutionalist* (Augusta GA), 10 April 1863, 1.

Varhola, Michael O. *Life in Civil War America.* Cincinnatti OH: Family Tree Books, 2011.

Ward, Geoffrey C. *The Civil War: An Illustrated History.* New York NY: Alfred A. Knoph, 1990.

Wright, John D. *Language of the Civil War.* Westport CT: Oryx Press, 2001.

Index

Index